The French gave us the term 'bourgeois', and then proceeded to argue endlessly about what it meant – 'of or pertaining to the French middle classes', according to the OED. But it is not a simple matter of social class. Béatrix Le Wita sets out to demonstrate that to be bourgeois one must master a system of words, gestures and objects that define a way of life, a particular culture. This requires the exercise of self-control and the ritualisation of daily routines. The bourgeoisie must furnish their rooms in just the right way, dress just so, tactfully invoke family history and custom. This witty, observant ethnography decodes the culture that dominates France.

The collection *Social anthropology of France* publishes research undertaken in the study of French society and culture under the patronage of the Mission du Patrimoine Ethnologique of the French Ministry of Culture and Francophony.

Funding for the English translation of this book was made available through a grant from the French Ministry of Culture and Francophony.

# FRENCH BOURGEOIS CULTURE

*Béatrix Le Wita*

TRANSLATED FROM THE FRENCH BY

*J. A. Underwood*

CAMBRIDGE
UNIVERSITY PRESS

EDITIONS DE
LA MAISON DES SCIENCES DE L'HOMME
PARIS

Published by the Press Syndicate of the University of Cambridge
The Pitt Building, Trumpington Street, Cambridge CB2 1RP
40 West 20th Street, New York, NY 10011–4211, USA
10 Stamford Road, Oakleigh, Melbourne 3166, Australia
and Editions de la Maison des Sciences de l'Homme
54 Boulevard Raspail, 75270 Paris Cedex 06

Originally published in French as *Ni vue ni connue: approche ethnographique de la culture bourgeoisie*
by Fondation de la Maison des Sciences de l'Homme, Paris 1988
and © Fondation de la Maison des Sciences de l'Homme

First published in English by Editions de la Maison des Sciences de l'Homme and Cambridge University Press 1994 as *French bourgeois culture*

English translation © Fondation de la Maison des Sciences de l'Homme and Cambridge University Press 1994

Printed in Great Britain by Bell and Bain Ltd., Glasgow

*A catalogue record for this book is available from the British Library*

*Library of Congress cataloguing in publication data*

Le Wita, Béatrix.
[Ni vue ni connue.]
French bourgeois culture / Béatrix Le Wita; translated from the French by J. A. Underwood.
    p.    cm.
Includes bibliographical references and index.
ISBN 0 521 44099 8. ISBN 0 521 46626 1 (pbk.)
1. National characteristics, French.  2. Middle classes – France – Social life and customs.  I. Title.
DC34.L4    1994
944–dc20    93–29766    CIP

ISBN 0 521 44099 8 hardback
ISBN 0 521 46626 1 paperback
ISBN 2 7351 0575 X hardback (France only)
ISBN 2 7351 0576 8 paperback (France only)

# CONTENTS

# ILLUSTRATIONS

Photographs 1, 4, 5, 9, 10, 11, 12, 15, 16, 18, 24, 26, 30, 31, 33 and 35 by Hugues Langlois. Photographs 2, 13, 14, 17, 25, 29, 32 and 34 by Jean-Michel Labat. Photograph 3 by André Pelle.

# INTRODUCTION

The bourgeoisie is always a copy of the court, said the seventeenth-century burlesque writer Paul Scarron, and French dictionaries, anxious to pass on the national heritage, have echoed him ever since. So be it. Three centuries on, however, we can presumably credit bourgeois culture with a degree of autonomy. Moreover, surely the bourgeois themselves lay claim to a culture nowadays, asserting their right to a separate identity? In fact, this long-drawn-out process of legitimation is not so very different, in terms of how it has happened, from the one that governed the 'making' of the nobility.

Let us not forget that, in France, the word *noblesse* did not supplant *gentilhomme, magnat* or *riche homme* until quite late on, namely in the first half of the fourteenth century. In the eleventh century, reference to one's ancestors did not define this wealthy personage. Horizontality only gradually gave way to verticality (G. Duby; see references, p. 162). Generally speaking, historians all agree on the extreme diversity of the nobility, even if socially its members very soon came to feel that they belonged to an immutable, hereditary body (Contamine 1976).

In the 1950s the French bourgeoisie too endowed itself with genealogical albums. In the process it was able to take stock of its own legitimacy, one based not on blood but on antiquity. Moreover, such genealogies began to be drawn up at the point where a certain continuity of bourgeois status made itself felt. The path from labourer to chairman of the board of a major company would seem to take us some way from the privilege of birth or hereditary quality. It is not the labourer that is important, however, but the three or four generations preceding the chairman of the board. Manufacturers, persons of private means, graduates of the *grandes écoles*,[1] the sequence of one's ancestors establishes one's legitimacy. 'Breeding' is replaced by 'civilisation'. Nowadays these 'legitimately' ancient families no longer necessarily occupy the seats of power. They are left with their quality of being civilised. And the bourgeois fits the definition of the cultural heir in that the idea of superior competence does not inhibit him:

[1] France's university-level colleges specialising in professional training [Tr.; footnotes and parentheses in square brackets are contributed by the translator].

I

An heir is someone who knows there are no mysteries: he assumes he is capable of doing as much as his parents managed to do and, had there been mysteries, his parents would have had access to them. (Veyne 1983)

Despite their diversity, then, these men and women recognise one another in a culture that is their own. That culture has long been a butt of caricature. Neither nobleman nor rustic, the bourgeois is somewhere in between, average, mediocre. Taken literally, that would make the bourgeois the man in the middle, his ecological niche this fine balance between extremes (the social metaphor of a law of physics, perhaps?). On the analogy of the balance, the bourgeois tends always to return to the middle position. It is a delicate, unstable situation, with the attraction of opposite poles giving rise, retroactively, to an attraction towards the centre.

We shall seek to give an account of this 'middleness', placing the emphasis on the trivial details that make what Foucault called the man of modern humanism (Foucault 1975).

The bourgeoisie eludes any kind of categorisation. Just when you think you have it, it slips through your fingers. Just when you feel you can put a name to it, it defies definition. To tackle these constant evasions and construct a problematics, we had to start from the word. Analysing the definitions of *bourgeoisie* and *bourgeois* in various [French] dictionaries suggested certain lines of thought. Oddly, all definitions of the words appear to involve some kind of wilful misrepresentation. Noting this malevolent eye that French society casts on a part of itself, we went on to examine the circumstances that such denigration has in its sights. What factors does this misrepresentation feed on? Paradoxically, the answer brought out certain values that together make up a culture. The task narrowed down to giving an account of that culture by studying the individual bourgeois. How, in short, does a person become a bourgeois? Is it enough to be born one, or does a person have to learn?

Seeking to ascribe a specific culture to the bourgeoisie would be hugely presumptuous without some very strong reference to the limitations of the present work.

Firstly, this is a personal journey through what for the author is unknown territory. The methodological approach gives some indication of the nature of that ignorance in a society in which the different social groups nevertheless rub shoulders with one another. The bourgeois are not packed into a corner of the *seizième* [Paris's wealthy sixteenth district]. However, to find some it was first necessary to meet some. The process was complicated by the fact that those who agreed to act as intermediaries with their peers belonged for the most part to the world of academic research. But getting to know a handful of people who admit to being 'bourgeois in inverted commas' is not the same as penetrating their family, social and cultural sphere and even less the 'milieu' from which they come and of which they form part.

1  The silverware

Flaubert's 'the bourgeois thinks in a low fashion' satisfies them completely. 'Low fashion?' said the solicitor, 'that rules me out, then!' (Berl 1931)

There are those who will be shocked by this mention of 'milieu', my academic intermediaries first among them, because for ages now cultural spaces have had to be thought of in terms of relationships, interpenetrations, resistances and borrowings rather than in terms of milieu, which is a product of the illusion of a certain closedness on the part of social groups or cultures. But my informants will also be shocked. The bourgeois refuse to be categorised. Even if they do, in passing, talk about 'our milieu', they will declare that they are 'open to others' or 'just like everyone else'. A person is always somebody's bourgeois:

The word bourgeois has, for the bourgeois, become an insult. They want a definition that has a splendid revolving-door at the exit complete with both automatic door-stopper and footman. Flaubert's 'the bourgeois thinks in a low fashion' satisfies them completely. 'Low fashion?' said the solicitor, 'that rules me out, then!' (Berl 1931)

However, the existential reality of an original milieu compelled recognition right from the start of the investigation in terms of the décor of large apartments, collections of ducks or onyx eggs, vast and ancient family seats, paintings and ancestral portraits on the walls, the ritual of tea in the drawing-room, the inevitable silverware, strolls in the garden, the life-style of these urbane men and women who converse with such subtlety or such irony, seeking all the time to control the conversational game, mentioning the Xs or

2 The ducks

'The two finest are the Korean duck and the Mexican silver duck. This collection was started about fifteen years ago. I'm bored with it, I'm collecting frogs now' (Mrs O. junior).

the Ys as if it went without saying that the investigator would know them. The individual disappears, swallowed up in a dense network of family and social relationships. Here the pronoun 'I' is little used; a royal 'we' indicates simultaneously membership of a group and the distance that lies between the speaker and the investigator.

This being 'outside' enables the investigator to recognise as distinctive the signs that separate him from the people being studied. But it may also lead him to exaggerate certain characteristics and as a result gain a somewhat naïve view of what he is observing. It is a familiar pitfall in ethnographic research, and every researcher will be used to sorting this one out for himself.

Here, however, everything is different. Anyone can ask the ethnographer to justify himself. On the basis of the knowledge that in varying degrees everybody may have of the subject, they will quibble about what he had seen and heard. The break with common parlance is perhaps more difficult in relation to this object than in other areas.

The first question (and it is an urgent one) is: which bourgeoisie are you talking about? The diversity and complexity of this social group suggest a medley of possible behaviours. The individuals picked out here can only represent tiny segments of the spectrum of bourgeois variety. So who will those individuals be? The answer, in common parlance, is men and women of all ages belonging to what is ordinarily termed the 'middle and upper bourgeoisie' of Paris. One further detail: they are Catholic. Some will seize on this (albeit very loose) demarcation in order to validate and at the same time restrict what will be set out in the course of this study. Others will be happy to ignore such arbitrary classifications. The aim of the study is to give an all-round cultural meaning to the term 'bourgeoisie', above and beyond the inevitable categorisations into *grande*, *petite*, middle, provincial, Jewish, Protestant, old, new, lower, upper and the rest. In fact, all these preconceptions have to do with the elusiveness of the object, as mentioned earlier.

To give an account of some of the factors peculiar to this bourgeois culture, it seemed appropriate to look at the forms of education that appoint an individual to the bourgeois state. One is born a bourgeois, yes, but one also learns to become one. Being born a bourgeois means entering an already existent culture with decipherable values or models. Becoming a bourgeois means enjoying the socially inherited ability to control those schemata and in so doing reproduce them. It is a further instance of the fundamental ambiguity of the notion of culture, which is a state but at the same time is also a process of socially influenced individual acquisition. The distinguishing feature of the bourgeois would thus be to stress or at least not to leave to chance the need for the heir actively to take possession of the values of the group. In fact, the educational concern turns that need into a categorical imperative: a person must already be a bourgeois in order to become one. An attention to detail, a certain self-possession or controlled introspection, and what almost amounts to a ritualisation of everyday practices constituting the passage from the private sphere to the public sphere would seem to characterise this culture that is conceived and experienced as something that goes without saying, the indispensable minimum required to rise above the state of nature.

From learning to acquisition, we shall also be looking at the role and symbolic importance that this social group attaches to the genealogical principle. By arranging the generations in order and giving each individual his place, genealogy makes a title of social function, thereby transforming it into privilege.

At the present stage of this investigation, many aspects will be merely touched on or suggested. The fact is, the conceptual foundations themselves need to be constructed. Although the bourgeoisie has been studied fairly extensively by both French and English-speaking historians, their concern has always been to pin it down at a particular moment of its history in relation to the development of the society they are studying. It is difficult, in this context, to identify the distinguishing features of a bourgeois culture over the long term. We shall discover, in fact, how historians are themselves put in the position of seeing the bourgeois slip away beneath the reality they are analysing.

As for the conceptual referents used in the economic and political sciences, they are no help at all. Notions of privileged or ruling classes, élites or sub-élites, merely fragment this group *ad infinitum*, increasing the opacity of the object. The bourgeois vanishes behind all these labels, all these layers of dissection, as it defies all chronological limits that are drawn too tightly.

To establish a specific, overall vision of the bourgeoisie, it was necessary to free it from the shadows cast by two reductive representations. One of these sees the bourgeoisie as a willing victim of the aristocracy; the other invariably describes it as a shameless exploiter of its fellows. This fixing of representations in the collective imagination stems from the very fact that the bourgeoisie has always claimed to base its social order on the principle of universality. As Friedrich Engels wrote:

We have seen how the French philosophers of the eighteenth century, the men who paved the way for the Revolution, appealed to reason as the sole judge of everything that existed. It was necessary to set up a rational state, a rational society; anything that contradicted eternal reason must be ruthlessly exterminated. We have also seen that this eternal relationship was in reality nothing more than the idealised under-standing of the citizen of the middle class, whose development in fact made him a bourgeois. (Engels 1973)

However, not everything was reasonable. And for a long time bourgeois culture found itself reduced to the economic and social function that a triumphant section of the bourgeoisie occupied for part of its history. It is at this level that we should reintroduce (with a view to transcending) the notion of milieu and observe how a cultural model is constructed out of borrowings and rejections, spreading in a thousand ways right through the social fabric. This very special position of the bourgeoisie as object complicates the question of its legitimacy in the discipline of anthropology itself. Certainly, it is no part of the tradition of anthropology to study a dominant group. On the contrary, the ethnology of modern societies shows a fascination with the local, often focusing for preference on the strata that, socially and culturally, are the farthest removed from the observer.

Consequently, the biggest problem in the present study lay in the play of looks between investigator and informants, with its concomitant risk of always thinking in the categories of knowledge produced by the group being observed. The object, the problematics, the whole approach made this investigation a product mid-way between sociology and ethnology. Neither discipline is going to be satisfied, and both must accept a degree of epistemo-logical blurring.

However, one question arises that would place the novelty of such an investigation project in perspective. It has been centuries since anyone shouted: 'Death to the bourgeois!' and many years (something like a hundred) since sociologists, historians and political scientists talked in prophetic tones of the death of the bourgeoisie. Yet it so happens that for the last few years (triggered by the bicentenary of the French Revolution, possibly?) the bourgeois, echoing the aristocrats, have been noisily laying claim to their own moral and cultural order. Surely this crystallisation around their manner of being and the kind of exhibition to which it has given rise (namely a spate of autobiographical success stories) really are symptomatic of their imminent disappearance? A swan song, as it were. In which case, studying the bourgeoisie of today is perhaps almost in the nature of an ethnographic emergency . . .

Behind these alarmist prophecies, regarding which younger-generation bourgeois evince a high degree of sensitivity, there is the ultimate question of the real attenuation of privileges. Demographic upheavals are putting pressure on and radically modifying the conditions of transmission of property. Today's heirs wait longer and in greater numbers than before. Meanwhile, freed from the shameful shadow of capital, they are able at their leisure to develop and recognise their cultural values and (why not?) snare the ethnologist in their nets!

# 1

## THE INVESTIGATION

It is 4.30 in the afternoon in the rue Cler in Paris's seventh district, and that woman is certainly one (navy loden coat, court shoes, little shoulder bag slung across her back). So is she (no doubt about it: soft black-leather coat with a lambswool lining, open to reveal a woollen roll neck). Both women, willy-nilly, evoke the word 'bourgeois'. Their air of neutrality, limited range of dress, certain shared emblematic details (court shoes, scarf, bag, ring) are so many tangible elements that the practised eye will recognise but that in the absence of more conspicuous clues will pass unnoticed. They may not evoke the word 'bourgeois' for everyone. And even if they did, not everyone would perhaps agree on what they had seen.

However, before juggling with these cultural schemata, it was necessary to pass through stages full of doubts and uncertainties and dominated by the question of the Other. Underlying many of the obstacles to observing everyday practices is this undeniable social fact: private life, in our society, is that which is legally entitled to escape outside scrutiny. According to the *Littré* dictionary, it is not even permissible to 'discover and publicise what takes place in a person's house' (Duby 1985). In other words, the very definition of the adjective 'private' precludes what to the ethnologist is a familiar practice. The situation is paradoxical, to say the least, and not without a certain ambiguity. In time you contrive to get round this sort of difficulty, even if a vague feeling of committing an offence still persists in your heart of hearts. On the other hand, forming a clear analysis of what goes on between the investigator and his subjects in the fieldwork situation is no easy task. It means, in fact, considering the investigative situation as being in itself a social fact or, to borrow a definition from the ethnomethodologists, a practical accomplishment making use of lay expertise and procedures. It would clearly be naïve to suppose that informants are capable, during interviews, of disregarding their own 'methodology'. Coulon uses the term 'lay methodology' to mean 'what is natural for the ordinary actor, the way in which he combines and permutates his natural assumptions in interactions in which he becomes involved with his peers' (Coulon 1986).

During this study I was led to observe, for example, that bourgeois culture is based on a conception of otherness in which precisely this question of the

3 A bourgeois silhouette?

A certain neutrality, subtle emblematic details, each one perceptible to the trained eye.

other person is, as we shall see, resolved before it has even been posed. In the circumstances, it is difficult not to wonder about the effects of this 'natural assumption' on the very course of interviews that arbitrarily place the person approached in the position of being an Other. It is a situation that, for the bourgeois of either sex, is socially unusual. So all my informants reacted in such a way as to reach a practical resolution of this social and cultural inversion occasioned by the investigation. Depending on the interpretative faculties of those involved, various procedures were used.

The first has to do with the question of identity: the informant wishes to know to whom he is talking. His concern is no more to become acquainted with the investigator than it is to show interest in (in this case) her professional qualifications. The informant simply wants to know whether the person in front of him belongs to his world or not. The trouble is, in his world that question does not arise: one usually knows whom one is dealing with. The informant proceeds to resolve this problem by asking questions about the links between the investigator and the intermediary: 'You must know Julie's grandmother, then?', 'You've surely visited their family seat?' and so on. The informant is looking for clues that will indicate the degree of familiarity or intimacy that the investigator has with 'his people'.

Another strategy is for the informant to employ humour to show (as may be done at any time) that he is aware of falling in with a curious game. In this way he contrives to put a distance between himself and what he says, or between him and the investigator.

A third method, finally, is for the informant to embody, for the duration of the interview, one of the possible representations of the bourgeoisie (historical, moral, virtuous, austere, urbane, cultivated, industrial, etc.). This is how those informants behaved who, without knowing why, felt embarrassed at having to talk about themselves. Because in their world it goes without saying that one does not push oneself forward. So in the very mechanics of the encounter these men and women brought their own reflexive, interpretative capacity into play. They sought to limit the disorder occasioned by an abnormal situation, that of being an Other to the extraordinary extent of being capable of forming an object of observation.

## The sample

Unlike a previous experiment of mine where I had used the door-to-door method (Le Wita 1984), here I was obliged to fall back on intermediaries in the form of friends or professional colleagues. There would have been no point at all in ringing the doorbell at random on, say, the third floor of 27 boulevard Delessert in the sixteenth district – and for one obvious and disturbing reason, namely that there is no guarantee a bourgeois family would be living there. So it was necessary to ask for informants. Some of these admitted to being bourgeois and were in little doubt, during the project, as to the difficulty of the undertaking. Consequently, everything began with a discussion about words. Although the terms 'bourgeois' and 'bourgeoisie' were understood favourably by the intermediaries, who were familiar with the purpose of my research, they were criticised from the outset by my informants-to-be. Invariably, the initial telephone contact was taken up by a discussion of the usage and meaning of these words. The informants approached were fearful of exposing themselves to caricature, this being an exercise that, though implicitly accepted at the level of social representations, is considered intolerable as soon as it touches the personal sphere. As we have seen, that raised the question of the position they could properly adopt in order to play this curious game.

*Mrs Arnold A.*

Mrs Arnold A. comes of a family of the industrial bourgeoisie whose wealth dates from the second half of the nineteenth century. The intermediary, a professional colleague, belongs to the family but was not an informant. Mrs Arnold A., aged 88, delightfully cultured and gently authoritative, was introduced as the repository of the family memory and guarantor of the transmission of the signs and symbols that constitute membership of the bourgeoisie. The investigation progressed no farther in this family. It proved impossible to contact other members of it, as had been planned. My brief integration in the life of this group had become an embarrassment.

The interest of the lengthy interviews punctuated by luncheons and teas that I had with Mrs Arnold A. lies in the panoramic vision that they provided of bourgeois society between the wars. At the time of the study, Mrs Arnold A. was living at the family seat some 80 kilometres outside Paris. Returning on the train one day, I made the following note: 'There's something wrong. Mrs Arnold A. never says I. She speaks of family and milieu without distinction.' So from my very first contact with the bourgeois milieu I was aware of the existence of an 'I' caught up in a dense, complex network of family and/or social relationships.

Apart from the interest of the interviews, my informant told me about the technological and industrial history books that recorded the principal discoveries made by her ascendants. She further drew my attention to 'libraries', even suggesting that I read the work of an author who had had a decisive influence on her, namely Rudyard Kipling.

Mrs Arnold A. embodied a triumphant bourgeoisie that, however, belongs to the past: tennis, sailing, regattas, arranged marriages, the heroism of the men of her family through two world wars, duets at the piano ...

## The Charles B. family

Here the intermediary was also an informant. Mr Charles B. junior, a personal friend, belongs to a family of judges. Aged 38, he is a newspaper proofreader, ghost, occasional journalist and writer (largely unpublished). At the time of the study he was living with a woman, a freelance journalist, who was not a member of the bourgeoisie. They had a 7-year-old daughter and lived in the thirteenth district. Today Mr Charles B. is separated from his partner. Numerous lunches and dinners extended our three morning-long interviews. What did Charles B. retain of his bourgeois origins? Answering that question was the guiding thread running through his account: a childhood, an immense distinction in his fringe existence, a past heavy with family history.

During our interviews I was able to consult the archives of his mother's family, a Camus novel in which a member of his kindred appears, a bulletin of the Court of Appeal (Formal Hearing) featuring a funeral oration for one of his uncles, his mother's family tree, a 1950 issue of the journal *Orient-Occident* mentioning a maternal cousin. Above all Mr Charles B. junior got me to read some of his semi-autobiographical private writing. He also allowed me to meet his father, whom he had not seen for some years.

Mr Charles B. senior, aged 70, is an estate administrator. We met in his chambers and spoke for three hours. His gracious reception of me did nothing to conceal his extreme reluctance to take part in the investigation. His contribution consisted mainly in a wealth of detailed information about Parisian solicitors and valuers.

## The Laure C. and Jean-Baptiste D. families

The young woman who was my intermediary for both of these families is a personal friend. On her father's side she comes of a family of lawyers. Her father is currently a director of one of the fifteen largest companies in France. Her mother's family belongs to the top wine-growing bourgeoisie (the 'aristocracy of the cork', as they call themselves). This friend served as intermediary with two of her relations. She was and still is a valuable informant.

*The Laure C. family* Laure C. junior belongs to the very highest reaches of the bourgeoisie. Her family, once a household name, owned one of the foremost industrial empires in France. This first informant (Mrs Laure C. junior) is a childhood friend of the intermediary: they knew each other at school (Sainte Marie; see below, p. 18). A 27-year-old architect, she was married to 'an aristocrat' who worked as a craftsman bookbinder. They lived in Belleville [north-east Paris] and had a daughter aged 2. We had a total of twelve hours' interview time at her home both during the day and evenings. Today Laure C. junior is divorced and lives in the more fashionable Neuilly. She was to be an essential intermediary for the study of the Sainte Marie colleges.

At the outset Laure C. junior gave me a copy of the history of the family written by a historian as well as two family trees. She also introduced me to her mother, a high-ranking OECD official aged 56 and the widow of an international lawyer. The first interview with the mother took place at her office, the second over dinner at her home in the sixteenth district.

Lastly, Mrs Laure C. junior introduced me to her 75-year-old grandmother, with whom I talked for several hours at her home, also in the sixteenth district.

The modesty of the mother's and grandmother's accounts was in inverse proportion to their family's fame. Speaking of their relations, all they said was quite simply that they were 'civilised people'.

*The Jean-Baptiste D. family*  Mrs Jean-Baptiste D. 53, agreed to meet me for a single interview on condition that we did not talk about her in-laws. They belong to the top industrial bourgeoisie (on a par with the family of Laure C.) and are anxious to 'avoid any publicity'. Mrs Jean-Baptiste D. stipulated her conditions when we met initially in a Paris café. We subsequently had a two-hour conversation at her mother's home in the sixth district rather than at her own (in Neuilly). Mrs Jean-Baptiste D.'s family consists of men of letters, judges and high-ranking civil servants and is fourth-generation Parisian.

I was not able to meet Mrs Jean-Baptiste D.'s mother, who was unwell at the time. In fact, Mrs Jean-Baptiste D. herself only agreed to see me out of friendship for the intermediary's family.

Mrs Jean-Baptiste D.'s contribution was in part bibliographical (I should read *Les Boussardel* by Philippe Hériat)[1] and in part methodological (I should make inquiries about buying a plot at the Père-Lachaise cemetery).

## The Emilie E. family

The intermediary in this case is an acquaintance of mine who belongs to the recent bourgeoisie. Her father used to have a responsible job with a stockbroker; her husband is a bank manager. This intermediary put me in touch with the family of her sister's mother-in-law.

Mrs Emilie E. senior (grandmother), aged 75 and living in Neuilly, is descended from a line of *rentiers* [persons of private means] domiciled in the capital but originally wine-merchants in the Bordeaux region. Her late

[1] A 'sub-Balzacian' social chronicle published in three volumes between 1939 and 1957, Hériat's novel traces the fortunes of four generations of a bourgeois family.

husband managed a medium-sized business based in the provinces. We had four conversations at her home, totalling about four hours. Mrs Emilie E. deliberately presented herself in the slightly flippant guise of a social butterfly.

Her contribution: literary references (Simone de Beauvoir, the sociologist and economist André Siegfried) and a number of books on right-wing intellectuals of the inter-war period. She gave me a copy of her family tree.

She also put me in touch with one of her granddaughters, whom she thought the 'most up in genealogy' and the best repository of the 'family memory'. This (paternal) granddaughter belongs to a family of the upper financial bourgeoisie related by marriage to the aristocracy.

After losing her father, this Mrs Emilie E. (the granddaughter) started in the bank, right at the bottom. She was 21 years old and lived in Neuilly. We had fifteen hours' interview time at her home, mornings and afternoons. She contributed family trees on her father's side.

She made several attempts to introduce me to her mother, who had remarried. The mother always put off the meetings, pleading personal reasons, so it seemed best not to insist.

The granddaughter did very kindly introduce me to the 80-year-old former governess of her father's family. I learned during our five-hour conversation that this woman came from a 'good family': her maternal grandfather had taught at a prestigious private school (Janson de Sailly), and her maternal great-grandfather had also taught at a high level. On her father's side they were all solicitors; a first cousin had been a governor of the Banque de France.

Following the death of her father when she was only 17, this woman had decided to get a job. She became a tutor and governess. She went to work for the Emilie E. family in 1938 to teach the boys reading and arithmetic. 'There were also two English nannies', she told me, 'whose main job was to teach the language and good manners.'

### The Grégoire F. family

Intermediary: a lawyer couple, both friends of mine. The man's father, a professor of law, was the first 'bourgeois' in the family, the grandparents having belonged to the commercial *petite bourgeoisie* [lower middle class). The woman's father is a high-ranking civil servant, and her mother's family owned a medium-sized business in the provinces. My lawyer friends introduced me to Mr Grégoire F., aged 39, an assistant public prosecutor. Grégoire F.'s father, now retired, had been prosecuting counsel at the Paris Court of Appeal and the first member of the family to have a job that provided access to the bourgeoisie. However, Mr Grégoire F. defined himself as a representative of an administrative bourgeoisie rather than one of birth.

Mr Grégoire F. became an assistant public prosecutor after a disappointment: 'With a cooking diploma, I was taken on as a waiter.' His brother had gone into the law after taking a diploma in boilermaking (their father, now retired, was involved in the professional training of solicitors). Only 'our sister gave full satisfaction', becoming a pharmacist and marrying a dentist. Yet Mr Grégoire F.'s father, as we have seen, had been a high-ranking official at the Paris Court of Appeal, his paternal grandfather had been a postmaster, and his paternal great-grandfather had been a schoolteacher. The whole family lived in the provinces and exemplified a perfect republican line and the kind of social advancement proposed by the nineteenth-century statesman and father of the French Republic, Adolphe Thiers. So why did Mr Grégoire F. refuse to call himself bourgeois?

I'm an assistant public prosecutor. That's the administrative bourgeoisie: one of the highest-paid public offices. You finish off the trousers of a suit with the jacket of another. However, it's a job that carries a certain social prominence, especially in the provinces. In Paris it is anonymous, and to be bourgeois you have to marry the girl who will bring you the apartment and all the rest.

Mr Grégoire F.'s father married the daughter of a provincial underwriter. As for Mr Grégoire F. himself, he is divorced from a woman engineer and is in his second marriage – to an 'adult-education teacher'. He said during our first interview: 'So far as marriage is concerned, clearly I'm not bourgeois.' We had two meetings in his office at the Palais de Justice.

My intermediary for the Louis G. and Georges H. families was an architect friend from a lower-middle-class family. In professional contact with people who belong to the bourgeoisie, he introduced me to two of his clients.

*The Louis G. family*

This family owns a (secular) private school on the outskirts of Paris. For the last four generations, ownership and management of the school have been handed down from father to son-in-law and then from father to daughter. With Mr Louis G. (the grandson), a bachelor architect of 27, we had two interviews, both over dinner, once at my home, the other time at his, lasting four hours each. With Mr Louis G. (the grandfather), aged 88, we had many long talks followed by lunch *en famille*. He had experienced the heyday of the family business and is currently witnessing its gradual decline, since the younger generation will not be 'taking up the torch' (numerous lunches during and after the study). The school is currently headed by the son and daughter of Mr Louis G. (the grandfather). For family reasons I was not able to talk to the son, but the 56-year-old daughter gave me four hours of her time.

Contribution of Mr Louis G. (the grandfather): magazines of his old scholars' association; private papers; many talks about pedagogy (the importance of Christian values in a liberal secular education).

This family is unique in my sample. The merging of workplace and living space highlights the problem of transmission and the division of roles and tasks between men and women.

*The Georges H. family*

The first member of this family to be interviewed was Georges H. junior, 38, whose occupation was hard to pin down (journalist, private adviser to a socialist minister, and, at the time of the study, unemployed following a six-month tenure of a responsible position in a nationalised company).

We had many long talks with Mr Georges H. at his home in the eighteenth district; I also talked to his wife, a lecturer at the Sorbonne, born in Paris but belonging to a family of the provincial upper bourgeoisie. The couple had two children, aged 9 and 6.

With Mr Georges H. senior, a 70-year-old retired company executive, we had three talks lasting four hours each at his home in the fifteenth district. His wife, aged 67, comes of a provincial-solicitor family going back five generations. We talked for four hours on two mornings at her home.

Contribution of Mr Georges H. junior: recommended reading of a decidedly anti-bourgeois nature (Fritz Zorn, *Mars en exil*, an autobiographical novel in which the author denounces his bourgeois upbringing, and Emmanuel Berl, *Le bourgeois et l'amour*, a derogatory pamphlet by a member of the liberal Jewish bourgeoisie).

Contribution of Mr and Mrs Georges H. senior: genealogical documents, the Bible; recommended reading: the *Memoirs* of André Maurois, the novels of Georges Duhamel.

This family occupies a very special place in the study. Father, son and mother joined in this 'curious game' with great kindness and great intelligence as well as with much humour. They were all confident of being bourgeois. But they were also aware of having a rather smaller fortune, rather fewer houses and a rather more modest degree of professional success than other members of their kindred. During the lunches that inevitably followed the interviews, Mr Georges H. senior enjoyed giving me 'object lessons' in table manners, showing in the process that he was capable of 'standing back' from the code.

There are very precise rules: you only eat with your right hand, with the bread on the left; you never dip your bread in the sauce; there are some foods you should stick with your fork and others not. If you need to pick something up, the handle of the spoon has to be above the hand, otherwise you're haymaking (a favourite expression of my mother's). Hands are placed on the table as far as the wrists only. Cheese must be cut according to its shape in such a way that you take as much rind as you leave.

Mr Georges H. junior also elected to toy with the boundaries: he was happy to be an informant but on condition that he could also ask questions. As a result,

during or outside the interviews we had long conversations sharing information. And 'distinction' in Bourdieu's sense (Bourdieu 1977) really did
become what was at issue in our interacting viewpoints. In short, father and
son wittingly made themselves the ethnologist's Others. Mr Georges H. senior
was my intermediary with the Pierre I. family.

## The Pierre I. family

Mr Georges H. senior put me in touch with a cousin on his mother's side,
defining the cousin's family as an example of 'bourgeois tradition and
refinement'. According to him, they should provide an 'ideal type' for my
study.

Mr Pierre I. senior, aged 60, was executive secretary of an industrial
company. He lived in a building in the sixth district that had been in his
family (of doctors and solicitors) for three generations.

We had 3 three-hour morning interviews with Mr Pierre I. senior at his
home. His wife came from a family of small industrialists that had likewise
been Parisian for several generations. We had two interviews with her lasting
some three hours. All the interviews were followed by lunch.

Contribution: Mrs Pierre I. lent me François Tollu's book, *Tableau d'une
famille parisienne*.

Mr Pierre I. senior introduced me to one of his sons, Mr Pierre I. junior,
aged 30, an engineer living in Versailles, married with three children. We had
a three-hour interview one Saturday morning. The wife of Mr Pierre I. junior
was present and took part in the interview. This is worth recording. In the
case of the other families I was always alone with the interviewee.

Is it true that, as Mr Georges H. senior had supposed, this family
constituted an 'ideal type'? In general terms the answer is yes. The Pierre I.
family is indeed 'the bourgeoisie' incarnate, occupying the median position of
the balance arm. The opposing forces enabling it to maintain that median
position are perceptible. Confident of their ancient bourgeois status, the Pierre
I. family are nevertheless afraid of seeing all that they have achieved placed in
jeopardy. While transmission to their children has gone without a hitch, Mr
and Mrs Pierre I. take very great care of their real-estate assets and of their
religious and cultural values. The children all own their own apartments,
they have sound professional careers, they have 'married well', the family
château has been re-roofed, yet still Mrs Pierre I. fears 'divorce' as a pervasive
social fact that may attack and disrupt her own family. As for Mr Pierre I., he
fears the 'social mixing' that makes it hard to control relationships and leaves
the door open to bad influences. In this family where 'everything ought to be
a matter of course', bourgeois values were constantly advanced in the
apparent hope of warding off the fear of failing to adapt to the times. Humour,
or toying with the boundaries (to be bourgeois, to have ceased to be

bourgeois, not to be bourgeois), were out of place with the Pierre I. family. It was in this sense, perhaps, that the family struck my intermediary, Mr Georges H. senior, as an 'ideal type': they were serious people.

### The Henry J. family

The intermediary, a personal acquaintance, was a branch manager of a major company. He put me in touch with someone he referred to as a 'colleague', now retired. All the intermediary knew about this colleague was the position he had occupied in the company and the fact that he lived in Paris. However, as observed in the case of the Grégoire F. family, this was an 'official' bourgeoisie. Mr Henry J., 65, belongs to a family of small craftsmen from a central quarter of Paris, the faubourg Saint-Antoine. Our single interview took place at his home in the twelfth district. The informant did not wish to discuss his family 'in detail' and would not let me meet one of his two daughters:

I had a bourgeois position, if you like. But I am not connected with the bourgeoisie. That's an outmoded criterion. Three-quarters of the company's executives were of modest origin, having come up through the ranks. For some years now, in France, people of courage and intelligence have been doing all right. A bourgeoisie of work is emerging, not necessarily descended from the old bourgeois families.

One of Mr Henry J.'s daughters is now a doctor and married to an officer; the other is a pharmacist, married to an engineer. One of them has now decided to draw up their family tree . . .

Aware of the fact that I was intruding upon the private lives of these men and women, struck by my discovery of a milieu in which the rules of etiquette are constantly present and implemented, I concentrated essentially on family histories and on the interactions that arose between observer and informant. This is why I refused, initially, to make notes about what I was observing (the décor of apartments, for example, or people's gestures and behaviour). During the second phase of my research, however, I made a special point of recording these visual impressions. This immersion in the bourgeois world enabled me gradually to put together a template more suited to my project of apprehending 'bourgeois culture'. I deliberately selected the world of the women of the Catholic bourgeoisie of Paris, and I decided to study the Sainte Marie colleges.

Most of the women educated at the Sainte Marie colleges, sometimes through several generations, do indeed belong to families of the Catholic bourgeoisie. This is a group that, we feel, enables us to apprehend the importance of Christian values within the French bourgeoisie. We shall also see how the relationship that has become established between the Sainte Marie colleges and the bourgeoisie is a source of the most intense irritation to the *demoiselles*, as the senior members of staff are called, all of whom belong to the apostolic community of Saint Francis Xavier.

Despite the recommendations of former pupils, the principal of the Sainte Marie college in Neuilly [known as Sainte Marie de Neuilly] would not tolerate a stranger in her establishment. Unable to write a monograph on the institution, I carried out a study of former pupils. Having kept in touch with my intermediary for the Laure C. and Jean-Baptiste D. families as well as with Laure C. herself, I was able, through these two women, to meet old girls of both Sainte Marie colleges (Sainte Marie de Neuilly and also Sainte Marie de Passy, which in 1970 became the Madeleine Daniélou Centre and moved out to Rueil).

Initially, the intermediaries were needed again. Some twenty interviews were conducted with women of various ages (from 18 to 48), including one *demoiselle* at Sainte Marie de Neuilly and a teacher at the Madeleine Daniélou Centre. Subsequently, Laure C. advised me to write to all the old girls of her year (1973), a list of whom she had kept. The list gave the names and addresses of 103 girls.

Giving Laure C. as a reference, I despatched 103 letters with a short questionnaire designed to find out what had happened to the young women in terms of marriage and career. Laure C. read and approved both letter and questionnaire.

Out of seventy-seven questionnaires that appear to have reached their destination (twenty-six came back marked 'not known at this address'), forty-nine answers were received. Forty young women agreed to meet me for an interview.[2]

The response was enthusiastic. All the young women showed a lively interest in a study bearing on their old school and recounted their experiences there with pleasure. My dealings with them were further facilitated by our belonging to the same generation as well as the same sex. I was thus able to share moments in their lives, sometimes spending several days in the family home. On such occasions I was able to listen as much as to observe and record their behaviour.

The study took place in Paris and its suburbs. So the territory cannot be spoken of as a precise geographical entity, except of course in so far as might be inferred from the correspondence between the social status of the informants and their places of residence. The older ones all lived in the sixth, seventh, eighth, sixteenth or seventeenth districts of Paris or in Neuilly. The younger ones lived in the western suburbs, with a few in the eighteenth or fifteenth districts. Modes of accession to the ownership of country estates accounted for this relatively broad spread.

My interviews involved something like a hundred men and women. Not

[2] See appendix for summaries.

4 Family strongholds

'The true bourgeois has two components: the power he wields personally and the power conferred by his family' (Mr Georges H. junior).

enough to claim to have covered the entire range of the bourgeoisie, but enough to be quite certain that repetition was beginning to appear. Far from being minor, the differences observed, whether at the level of wealth or at that of everyday custom, only brought out more clearly the significance of bourgeois cultural traits.

The very real methodological difficulty inherent in this type of investigation among well-to-do people lies essentially in the risk the researcher runs of being manipulated. In addition to their diplomas, the subjects possess a certain cultural capital and the ability to make conscious use of it. Anxious to control the representation they are about to give of themselves, they seek to dominate the ethnographic inquiry, for example by swapping the status of informant for that of questioner. Line of descent, genealogy and education are presented to the investigator as the pillars of the bourgeoisie. Mr Georges H. junior said quite baldly during one interview:

There is a historical bourgeoisie, it's the number of wing collars there are up above you. The true bourgeois has two components: the power that he wields personally and the power conferred by his family.

Granted, the 'indigenous' theory cannot be taken at face value. But an interview conducted with a subject who has read a lot of sociology puts the investigator in an unusual position, to say the least.

5  Smart districts

The subject's superiority will be a constant presence, unstated yet terribly insistent (the
boulevard Delessert in Paris's sixteenth district).

Virtually all anthropological research is in fact directed towards 'under-classes' or towards remote, foreign Others, not towards the upper classes of our own society. In the beginning the discipline seems even to have defined an Other for itself, a 'whole':

A person who belongs to the élite is not simply *homo duplex*, he is more than simply split within himself; he is, if I may be permitted the expression, 'divided': his intelligence, the will behind it, his reluctance to express his feelings, the way he keeps those feelings under control, his (often excessive) critical faculties prevent him from ever abandoning his whole awareness to the violent impulses of the moment ... *But it is not such men that we sociologists usually have to study. The common man is already split and has feelings: but he is not in control of himself.* The average person today – this is particularly true of women – and nearly everybody in archaic or backward societies is a whole: he is affected in his entire being by the least of his perfections or by the slightest mental upset. Consequently, the study of this 'whole' is of capital importance as regards everything that does not concern the élite of our modern societies. (Mauss 1968)

There is no doubt that studying members of the élite places the ethno-graphic investigator in a state of permanent tension in which his own position is open to question. The reason for this is that his subjects' 'superiority' will be a constant presence, unstated yet terribly insistent. It is extremely awkward for an investigator bristling with degrees to have forgotten his Latin, say, or not to know the author of the poem his interviewee is so good as to recite. However, the investigator does have one trump card: observing and listening to his subjects, he very quickly learns how to get out of these tricky situations by borrowing his subjects' cultural schemata. That is why, in order to give an account of this bourgeois culture, it was necessary to get used to seizing the gesture, toying with contradictions, thinking in terms of paradox, and having an eye for every detail, no matter how trivial it might seem.

However, studying the bourgeoisie through its ways and customs exposes the investigator to the risk of appearing frivolous as he makes a note of or draws attention to things that are 'common knowledge'. The bourgeois seeks to present himself as an 'average man' accessible to all, much as common sense is, in Descartes' ironic dictum, the 'most widely distributed commodity in the world'. His conspicuous lucidity upsets the rules of the game. For instance, his peculiar cultural characteristics, through always being pre-sented as universal, not to say natural, may cease to be perceived as distinguishing marks. It is in precisely such ways that the bourgeoisie contrives to remain invisible. Permanently under construction, it is con-stantly renewing itself, which means, as we shall see, that it eludes all definition.

# 2

## DEFINITION BY DEFAMATION

But what do you mean by bourgeoisie? How would you define it? Two identical, penetrating questions, two ritual objections that inevitably meet every attempt to stake out the territory for a study of the bourgeoisie. As if no use of the term *bourgeoisie* were conceivable without the firm foundation of a definition.

The words *paysan* (peasant, rustic), *ouvrier* (worker) and *noble* (nobleman) trigger no such demand. Mention *bourgeoisie*, however, and you will set off a chain reaction that is part fascination and part scientific scepticism. Any attempt to define the word is doomed to come up against complex opposition. The two ritual questions that open this chapter undermine 'your' answer before it is given. The fact is, that answer is penalised for bieng necessarily (indeed, inevitably) personal. A curious situation indeed, when subjectivity is offered both as a way out of the difficulty of demarcating a concept satisfactorily and at the same time as proof of the unscientific nature of what you are trying to do (Le Wita and Sjögren 1987 (a)).

### A story of words

Under the entry *bourgeois*, the authors of the Larousse dictionary, writing more than a century ago, in 1867, could not resist the temptation to quote 'Mr Nestor Roqueplan's witty sally' [Roqueplan was a well-known wit and dandy of the mid-nineteenth century; Tr.]:

What is a bourgeois? Such is the question more often avoided than dealt with on which it would not be inapposite to reach agreement. The first thing to note is that the absurd acceptance of the word bourgeois is peculiar to us French . . .

Molière's George Dandin, Sganarelle, and Jourdain, Henri Monnier's Prudhomme, the bourgeois of the artists and the little magazines, the fellow who came to embody the small-mindedness, dull-wittedness, and incoherent metaphors of a whole class of citizens who were naturally placed outside the army and the Church and to whom limits were assigned at the lower end in the urban and rural working populace and at the upper end in heaven knows what confused contemporary nobility, that fellow occurs only in our literature . . .

Why is it that the type is almost exclusive to French literature? Is he a mere convention, or did the model, if he is no more, ever exist at all?

. . . This sort of low punning at the bourgeoisie's expense gradually disappeared as 1789 approached.

The jokes resumed with the advent of fresh ideas in art and literature. And since alongside this purely intellectual movement a political movement emerged, the attacks were launched from these two diametrically opposing camps. Anyone not in favour of the new art and the new politics was dubbed bourgeois. The pattern of this figure was at that time complete. Complete entrenchment in certain selfish, mean-minded ideas, the pursuit of a middle-of-the-road art, a middle-of-the-road politics; the pretty and the graceful ousting the beautiful and the great, order and actuality supplanting progress and idealism, teasing and prattle taking the place of discussion, correctness that of vehemence, false elegance and mixed metaphors that of true style and consistent imagery – in a word, pretentious, stick-in-the-mud stupidity substituting for passion and originality.

Yes indeed, among the various effigies of human nature there are those that match such a portrait, but they no more belong to the bourgeoisie than to the nobility or the working classes. So why has the portrait been labelled bourgeois?

... It is not the bourgeoisie alone that accounts for the success of these ghastly portraitists for whom society ladies have been falling over themselves to sit. Where did they come from, almost without exception, the writers, artists, orators, philosophers, soldiers, and statesmen who raised this country to its present exalted position? They came from the bourgeoisie.

Still relevant today, Roqueplan's satirical words illustrate what Roland Barthes dubbed 'name defection' (*défection du nom*; Barthes, 1970). By depreciating the words *bourgeois* and *bourgeoisie*, individuals of that ilk are in effect forbidding you to call them such. The 'class' questions its own existence, imagines its own ambiguity.

Anyone who persists in trying to define the bourgeoisie sociologically is doomed, in fact, to seeing the reality observed disappear. It vanishes behind the socio-occupational statistics. In seeking to match it to terms as disparate as 'moneyed or privileged classes', 'upper classes', 'upper middle class', or plain 'middle class', we lose it altogether. We lose it again when we fall back on internal distinctions such as 'Parisian or provincial', 'industrial or financial', 'Catholic or Protestant', 'upper [*haute*] or lower [*petite*]', and so on. The multiplicity of directions leads only to a haemorrhage of meaning.

That is the reason why this whole piece of fieldwork started with a study of words, use of the terms *bourgeois* and *bourgeoisie* giving rise to problems both in the academic world (demands for a definition) and in the indigenous world (reactions of suspicion). Paradoxically, ethnographic observation did for its part offer an appreciable glimpse of the 'existential reality' of the bourgeoisie.

However, it having been impossible, all these years, to utter the word 'bourgeois' without clothing it in inverted commas, it seemed necessary to consult a few dictionaries for the various ways in which they deal with the word. In fact, no better epitome of the problems of lexicography could be found. Regarding the word as part of the stock vocabulary of the average speaker, dictionaries of language reflect its true function in spoken and written discourse. Fixed in accordance with conventional rules, the definition of the word is in this case the translation, in concise but explicit form, of all the semantic features contained within it.

It would be naïve to look in this direction for a definition of the bourgeoisie. Any such attempt would be doomed to failure. It is simply a question of recognising and seeking recognition for the words *bourgeois* and *bourgeoisie* as they are used.

Our intention is to look closely at the various wrappings, the various liveries in which these words have comed to be dressed up. As we do so, we shall find that beneath these alluvial strata the 'object' appears to elude us or rather to emerge into paradox.

The logical development of the dictionary definitions offers the spectacle of this kind of astute management juggling with etymological and historical factors, a shot at sociological reflection and the pejorative meaning. Our survey of dictionaries from *Trévoux* (1771) through *Bescherelle* (1864), the nineteenth-century *Larousse* (1867), and the twentieth-century *Larousse* (1961) to *Robert* (1967) and *Lexis* (1975) illustrates the view that French society takes and has taken of a part of itself.

No language is mere nomenclature. And concealed behind this story of 'words' is of course the symbolic apprehension of the reality they designate. The paradox here, however, is that the word never seems to be able to match the thing. To put it another way, *bourgeois* does not appear to mean *bourgeois*, as if everything were conspiring to produce a loss of meaning, a ban on use.

The semantic field occupied by the words *bourgeois* and *bourgeoisie* seems to be traversed by five main thoroughfares. First there is the principal avenue of every good dictionary, namely etymology. *Burger, burgis, bourg*: the *bourgeois* originates in the town. The second direction pursued by the definitions is the variety of possible acceptations (from the wealthy merchant to the person of independent means, passing by way of the good paterfamilias and not forgetting the owner of the means of production). The third theme concerns the bourgeoisie as intermediate class. Neither nobleman nor soldier, neither peasant nor worker, the bourgeois has enough trouble defining himself in isolation without the interference of these double negatives. The fourth avenue is a veritable nerve pathway running through all the others, namely the obligatory detour of the pejorative sense, the countless ways in which *bourgeois* is used as a vehicle of scorn and disparagement. Lastly, we shall see that the adjective *bourgeois* has [in French] its specific applications (to soup, to wine, to architecture, to families or suits), offering the spectacle of a true culture.

Analysing these five elements calls to mind the marionette character of la Mère Gigogne [our 'old woman who lived in a shoe'; Tr.]. From beneath the skirts of this giantess streamed a host of children. Similarly, as soon as you think you have isolated one meaning or one characteristic feature of the word *bourgeois*, you find it flanked somewhere else by a totally different acceptation or blurred by denigration. To illustrate this process, it will be a useful exercise to look at one definition in its entirely [or as nearly so as makes sense in translation]. Reading *Trévoux*, we shall see how, long before the nineteenth century, presentation and representation of the bourgeoisie flowed together as in a piece of fiction.

### The *Trévoux* definition (1771 edition)

Inhabitant of the town and middle class:

– One who ordinarily resides in a town and possesses a degree of rank mid-way between the Nobility and the Peasantry (Abbé Girard). True politeness is scarcely found except among courtiers and the principal Bourgeois of the major towns ... Voltaire, writing about Corneille's *Nicomède*, notes that this expression now has no place in noble style. It was accepted in Rome and still is in republics ... It has lost some of its dignity, possibly because we do not enjoy the rights it expresses. A Bourgeois in a Republic is usually a man who is capable of attaining employment: in a Monarchy he is a common man. The word is thus ironical in the mouth of Nicomède and in no way detracts from the noble assurance of his speech.
– This word comes from the German *Burger*, which means the same thing, or rather, according to Pasquier, it comes from the old word *bourg*, which meant a town.

Historical meaning: body of bourgeois people and people of the Third Estate:

– Bourgeois is also used as a collective noun signifying the collectivity or body of those who are called bourgeois in the true sense of the word ...
– Bourgeois also sometimes denotes all the people of the Third Estate, as distinct from Clergy and Gentlemen, who enjoy a number of privileges not enjoyed by the People. The burdens of State are borne by the Bourgeois ...

Also said in scorn:

– Bourgeois is also said in scorn to denote a man who is not a Gentleman or who has no wordly manners ...

Historical meaning and diversity of acceptations:

– A number of customaries call 'King's Bourgeois' people who have some privilege to plead only in the Royal Jurisdiction and to decline the Jurisdiction of the Lords: this is what happens in the Customaries of Troyes, Champagne, Chaumont, Sens, and Auxerre: it is also known as 'Right of Juror' [*droit de Juré*], because those who made themselves answerable to the King took an oath before the Judge Royal; and for that they paid a duty [*droit*] of six deniers per livre for movables and ten deniers for immovables; this was called 'right of Bourgeoisie' [*droit de Bourgeoisie*].
– ENFEOFFED BOURGEOIS, an inhabitant of a town where the Bourgeoisie, the Mairie, the Echevinage, and the Commune are held in feoff from the King; or from another lord (Ragueau).
– People are called King's BOURGEOIS who though living on seigniorial land, all of the inhabitants of which are serfs of the Lord ... are exempt from such servitude by virtue of their privilege, which excepts them therefrom and which in some places even excludes them from the Lord's jurisdiction and makes them answerable in the first instance to the Judge Royal.

– This privilege of royal BOURGEOISIE was introduced only for certain places in Champagne, where all the People are of servile rank, with the result that if some itinerant came to live in the territory of a Lord he would become his serf: as those who settle in some locality in that Province, to exclude themselves from servitude to the Lord of the locality, appeal to the King or his Officers, who give them letters of Bourgeoisie and royal protection.

## In the Naval sense:

– Bourgeois in the naval sense is the proprietor of a vessel, whether through purchase or because he had it built.

## Popular uses of the word:

– Bourgeois is what workers call the person for whom they are working . . . It is in this sense, contrasting Bourgeois and artisans, that the King says in the 1667 Ordinance, article XI: The Judges and the parties may name Bourgeois as experts; and where an artisan is involved in his own right against a Bourgeois, only a Bourgeois may be called on as an expert witness.

## Successive paraphrases: bourgeois house [*maison bourgeoisie*] and bourgeois family [*famille bourgeoise*]:

– BOURGEOIS (OISE) is also an adjective with the same meanings as it has as a noun. A bourgeois house is a house built simply and without splendour yet convenient and habitable; and it is also in contrast to Palace, hotel, and hut or peasant's or artisan's house. In villages, Bourgeois Houses are those owned by the Bourgeois of the nearby towns, as opposed to those of the inhabitants of the locality. The villages around Paris are full of bourgeois houses. A house or family is called bourgeois when it is not noble but is above artisan level in terms of its property and pursuits.

## Also said in scorn: bourgeois turns of speech, ways of behaving, airs:

– It is also used adjectivally in the other sense. That is utterly bourgeois (Molière). You must cut out your bourgeois – i.e. low and vulgar – turns of speech. He behaves in very bourgeois ways. You will see a bourgeois air enter this family that will not leave it for another ten generations. I have never seen a body composed of more bourgeois atoms (Molière, *Le Bourgeois gentilhomme*).

## Specific uses: bourgeois custody, bourgeois guard, bourgeois guarantee, bourgeois wine, bourgeois soup:

– Bourgeois custody is the name of a right laid down in the Paris Customary in imitation of nobiliary custody whereby fathers and mothers, grandfathers or grand-mothers are entitled to enjoy their under-age children's assets without rendering an account to them, maintaining them as they are and paying the personal debts on them.
– Bourgeois guard is the name given to the militia made up of the bourgeois who keep watch in some part of their town . . . A bourgeois guarantee is a good guarantee, easily discussed.
– Bourgeois wine is the wine that the Bourgeois of the city of Paris harvest from their vineyards and that they are entitled to sell from home by the jar. The expression is also used to refer to the unadulterated wine a person has in his cellar, as opposed to tavern wine. In the same vulgar sense people will speak of bourgeois soup, good soup . . .

The adverb: *bourgeoisement*:

– In a bourgeois manner, *Agrestius, simplicius, rudius*. He lives, speaks, and reasons *bourgeoisement*. At noon he dines *bourgeoisement*, with his family; but well and with an appetite.

Bourgeoise (fem.): Etymological element and historical meaning:

– *Jus civitatis*. The quality of being a citizen. The word presupposes a town and a society in which every individual is familiar with business, cherishes the good, and can expect to reach the highest rank. It is necessary to have resided for ten years in free towns to acquire right of Bourgeoisie and exemption from tallage. The right of Bourgeoisie in Rome or Roman Citizenship carried with it great advantages: it was even granted to foreigners. Sparta was so jealous of its citizenship that Herodotus remarked that it granted it to only two people . . . Frenchmen lose their French right of Bourgeoisie by settling in foreign countries; however, they recover it if they return to France (Piment in *Le Nouveau Practicien François*). See *Histoire de Lyon* by P. Meneftrier, p. 488, for the way in which Bourgeoisie must be asked for and granted.

– BOURGEOISIE, used also in collective terms of the whole body of the Bourgeois. *Cives*. The Bourgeoisie is under arms . . . The Bourgeoisie is always a copy of the Court (Scarron).

## The bourgeois and the town

*A meaning now lost and distorted*

We have seen how, etymologically, the word *bourgeois* is related to the word *bourg* (*burgeis* in the twelfth century; a market town). 'Citizen, inhabitant of a town' echoed the 1867 edition of *Bescherelle*. According to the dictionaries, historical developments of varying durations came to back up this etymological element. With the nineteenth-century *Larousse* (which admittedly aspired to encyclopaedic status) this original meaning is thus fleshed out with historical information recalling the various stages of development of small towns [*bourgs*] and municipalities [*communes*] in France.

BOURGEOIS (OISE), n. In his preface to the twelfth volume of the Edicts of the Kings of France, de Brequigny assigns the following origin to the word bourgeois. In the tenth century the name bourg was given to villages not enclosed by walls. The troubles that disturbed the period having forced people to enclose such dwellings within walls, they continued to be called bourgs. Eventually, by imperceptible degrees, the name was given only to localities enclosed by walls and so departed from its original meaning. The same thing happened to the word bourgeois, which at first was used to describe the inhabitants of villages whether open or enclosed. When the enclosed villages rose to the status of towns their inhabitants retained the name bourgeois. Finally, when such localities obtained privileges for their inhabitants as a body, the name bourgeois came to characterise individuals of that body to the exclusion not only of the inhabitants of non-privileged localities but even of those inhabitants of the privileged locality who had not been associated with the body to whom the privilege had been granted. This had the effect of narrowing the initial acceptation of the word bourgeois: originally, it had simply expressed an idea of place, and the idea of privilege was then linked to it (see BOURGEOISIE). A person who inhabits a town and enjoys certain special rights similar to rights of citizenship: the BOURGEOIS of Cracow made so bold as to close their doors to the conquerors (Voltaire).

To state the strict meaning, *Trévoux* uses the present tense ('one who ordinarily resides in a town') where *Bescherelle* employs the imperfect ('used to be said collectively of the whole body of the citizens or bourgeois of a town'). It is not without interest to note that we pass, through the examples we have chosen, from a Bourgeois of Paris (*Trévoux*) to a bourgeois in Switzerland (nineteenth-century *Larousse*): 'In Switzerland the word bourgeois still denotes the inhabitants of a town who are possessed of certain privileges and who constitute the bourgeoisie.' It is not part of our intention to submit these definitions to historical analysis. That has in fact already been done by Peronnet, who studied the words *bourgeois* and *bourgeoisie* through various editions of the dictionary of the Académie française. If we may borrow Peronnet's conclusions, as time went on the link between the word *bourgeois* and the town became archaic. From the nineteenth century, in fact, dictionaries tended 'to make *bourgeois* a word that was obsolete in France and only still in use abroad.' (Peronnet 1987).

The tendency also expressed the reduced share given to the etymological meaning. The *Robert* dictionary, for example, tucks this element of the definition away under the heading 'classical and literary'. The *Lexis*, for its part, abandons any historical reference and recalls the etymon in the most concise form possible: 'Bourgeois(e), adj., from Bourg'. In such ways the dictionaries take account of the desuetude into which the oldest meaning of the word has fallen so far as most speakers are concerned. And quite obviously few people nowadays will find that the word *bourgeois* suggests 'the inhabitant or privileged citizen of a town' (*Bescherelle*).

Here there will be some emphasis on the first of a long series of paradoxes. The fact is that this etymological meaning, which one might expect to be exempt from any interpretation of an ideological nature, is followed, in the event, by quotations that are definitely on the spiteful side. After giving the first meaning of the word, *Bescherelle* specifies that 'nowadays the word bourgeois is applied to people who live without doing anything, who consume without producing'. This is backed up by a quotation from the seventeenth-century critic Jean de La Bruyère: 'Do not speak to a great many BOURGEOIS of fallow land or staddles or stocks or aftercrops if you wish to be understood: such words are not, to their ears, French.'

The picture is much the same in the nineteenth-century *Larousse*, where it is embellished with two further quotations:

Well-to-do person who lives in town, as opposed to those who live in the country: Do not speak to a great many BOURGEOIS [etc.]. (La Bruyère)

A lover of gardening,
Half-bourgeois, half-boor. (La Fontaine)

Fancying oneself somebody is very common in France;
A man will pretend to be grand
And often be a mere bourgeois. (La Fontaine)

In *Robert* only the first La Fontaine quotation survives. In contrast to this dictionary's economical style, its presence seems contrived if not incongruous.

Bourgeois: ... Formerly. Citizen of a town or city enjoying privileged status. The bourgeois of a municipality. The bourgeois [burghers] of Calais. A wealthy bourgeois. – Person emancipated from the feudal jurisdiction of a lord.

> A lover of gardening,
> Half-bourgeois, half-boor.                                    (La Fontaine, *Fables*, IV, 4)

Reflecting an obsolete representation of the bourgeoisie, this quotation, which looks out of place, startles and challenges the reader. How are we to interpret these phrases evoking the link between the bourgeois and the countryside when what has just been spelled out is his link with the town?

### The bourgeois beyond the walls

Born of or in the town, inhabiting the town, the bourgeois was in fact defined as someone who was able (had been able from the outset) to detach himself from the town. In his portrait of a typical bourgeois of the sixteenth century, F. Braudel certainly mentions the economic aspect ('being relatively well-off') and the moral aspect ('living with dignity'), but he also speaks of the need 'to have purchased a few fields around the town' (Braudel 1979). If we look at the modern period, the purchase of estates seems to have been regarded by contemporaries and interpreted by many historians as the surest way of entering the nobility. The quotations from La Bruyère and La Fontaine would in that case express the contempt in which a society held one of its elements when that element sought at all costs to penetrate the body of the established élites. Hence the significance of the second La Fontaine quotation in the nineteenth-century *Larousse*: 'Fancying oneself somebody ...'

As soon as the bourgeois tries to build like his 'betters', he finds himself overshadowed by the nobility. He will never be a landed aristocrat. Hence his first antonym: nobleman. As a landowner, he can never do more than quietly, idly enjoy the delights of country life, knowing nothing of the land. Hence his other antonym: *paysan* [literally 'peasant', but a closer English equivalent to the French usage would be 'countryman']. Neither peasant nor nobleman, he is left with gardening, horticulture, a love of things rustic – pursuits that represent what has been called a 'projection, beyond the city walls, of a world derived from the town, drawing its vigour and refreshing its tastes in the town, fascinated by all the things expressed in the word "civilisation"' (Richet 1969). Granted, as Braudel points out, there is not a town in Europe whose money does not spill over into the surrounding countryside. But we know that the 'gardening' so mocked by La Fontaine was not always innocent of economic concerns. In

6  Old Adrien

'Leaves falling, mist over the pond, old Adrien planting tulip bulbs' (from a letter).

fact it was the object from the outset of careful management of land and its productivity. When Huppert imagines a conversation between Monsieur de Gouberville, a bourgeois by calling, and the sixteenth-century essayist Montaigne, he has the former expatiate volubly upon pigs – to the point of boring the famous thinker to death. However, the author goes on:

> Had a gentleman, accustomed to army camps and court life, lent an indulgent ear to what he was saying, he would have discovered little by little that that gentleman, far from being a simpleton, was on the contrary an expert who ran a vast agricultural business for profit, thus blending the work of agriculture with the spirit of the bourgeois. (Huppert 1983)

Having houses in the country meant being able to get hold of wheat, wood, poultry, pigs, fresh fruit, and so on. Nowadays, only isolated practices recall that kind of self-sufficiency. Come the dessert course, wrinkly apples, plums that are always slightly unripe or extremely overripe, or pears from the orchard will appear on the bourgeois table. All other types of fruit seem to be banned from the house. There is not one account, not a single private diary that does not recall the pleasure of whole afternoons spent munching fruit from the orchard. Never ask a bourgeois why it is always apples, pears or plums that are served. You will provoke either astonishment ('But aren't they the kinds of fruit people eat?') or some such reaction as this:

> Eating *one's own apples*: the pleasure of the familiar even on the table. Apples of known provenance ('the tree on the left as you come into the orchard', 'the old tree that fruits

so well'), untreated, stored on straw, their flavour and texture well known to everyone, their very faults endearing, intimate apples with wrinkles that do not spoil the way they taste, altogether unaffected, unpretentious apples, apples that speak of the seasons, the leaves falling, mist over the pond, old Adrien (or Jules) planting tulip bulbs, All Saints' Day and the young cousins who will be gone for the winter ... Sunday evening apples (the man's night off), grandmother's apples: essence of culture and memory, fruit steeped in the past and its green elysium[1] (playing croquet beneath the limes, reciting poetry, cousin Christine's breasts beginning to show, cold sheets and ancient lavatory, mass at eight in the cathedral crypt, the canons respectful, books banned ...). (extract from a letter)

Tracing the path of those apples, which are enjoyed both at the family seat and in the Paris apartments to which they are brought back and where they are savoured and distributed to those members of the family unable to 'go down' and pick their own, suggests that the bourgeois/town relationship should be approached by way of the country. In every sense, in fact. For many of the families that are now bourgeois originated in the country. This is the case with one branch of the L. family, for instance, whose ancestors were wine growers, husbandmen, farmers. 'Mind you', adds Grandma, whose account this was, 'these weren't casuals or day labourers. Nor were they landowners, that was not until the nineteenth century ...' The family was scattered among the villages of Burgundy.

One of them settled in A. at the end of the eighteenth century, they married and started a line ... At that time they were school rectors (or teachers in the nineteenth century) and wine growers, sometimes both at the same time. Some you find were coopers and tradesmen, even merchants (in the nearby town), and it was not until the end of the nineteenth century that they went to Paris to find wives. (Latour 1975)

So we cannot attribute the bourgeois/country link to a simple misunderstanding or to idle enjoyment, as the quotations from La Fontaine suggest. And the point of the references to Monsieur de Gouberville and the flavour of those apples is to remind the reader of a few fragments of a reality that the descriptions contrive to obscure.

The acquisition of lands, feoffs and country houses by the descendants of manufacturers and merchants has been seen almost throughout history as the stigma of social climbing. It seems the conquering bourgeois cannot be regarded in any other light than as an upstart. In a description of the social order as presided over by the nobiliary ideal, there is no place for the bourgeois, as we shall see. He is reduced to being merely a pale imitation of the nobleman. This representation was sometimes so prevalent as to take the place of an explanation. Thus Pourcher, for example, describing in minute detail the mechanics of the acquisition of lands in Lozère [southern central

---

[1] Cf. le vert paradis des amours enfantines ('the green elysium of childhood loves'), Baudelaire, Les Fleurs du mal, 'Moesta et errabunda' [Tr.].

France] by former manufacturers who had worked hard and saved hard, speaks of bourgeois folk as being 'haunted by nobiliary prejudice" (Pourcher 1987).

'Haunted by nobiliary prejudice': the whole question is summed up already at this etymological level of definition. If we agree to think of the bourgeois as having for a certain period of time been subject to the laws of a hierarchical society, does that mean we must reduce them generically or definitively to being mere imitators? Representations notoriously have a longer life-span than the realities that underlie them. And if the La Fontaine quotation struck us as being out of place in *Robert*, it is because it is only there to comply with a lexicographical tradition according to which some account must be given of a word's pedigree. Quoting La Fontaine was meant to make it possible to highlight the gap between the old usage of the word *bourgeois* and its current usage.

Such representations are no longer acceptable today, when ownership of a family seat [*maison de famille*] has come to represent a life-style where the marks of privilege are manifest.

## A certain life-style: the family seat

Estates, houses in the country, family seats, second homes – there are many ways of referring to the various dwellings of bourgeois families. 'They (the houses) reserve for a few privileged persons and their countless relations a portion of the glorious national territory' (Tollu 1972). And we are not talking about one house but several, some situated near the capital, others farther away.

This, spread across the members of a wider kindred, is the patrimony; it cannot be reduced to a single property, a single proprietor. As Tollu puts it:

There are ancestral properties, cousin properties, sister properties, and daughter properties for those who own no houses as yet but will do 'when our nephews and nieces have saved up'.

Each of the families studied did indeed own one or a number of homes situated all over France. At the time of our interviews, Miss Emilie E.'s paternal grandmother was bequeathing apartments in Neuilly, large tracts of land in the Morvan [eastern central France] and houses and land in Normandy. At the age of 22, Emilie was thus the owner of a small farm on the estate. One of her uncles inherited the stud farm and the château. Her grandmother on her mother's side for her part owned an estate in the provinces, an apartment in Neuilly, and a 'little place' in the Midi.

The maternal grandparents of Mrs Laure C. own an *hôtel particulier* [detached town house] and an apartment in Paris. Several houses in a village near Paris and a property in the Midi also belong to them. Through other

7  Family seats 1
Owning a family seat has come to represent a life-style where the marks of privilege are manifest.

genealogical lines Miss Laure C. may also come into an 'aunt' chalet in the mountains, a 'cousin' house in Arcachon, and so on.

Without anticipating the part played by these houses in sustaining and reproducing social and family history, we can say that they are regularly experienced as a great privilege, possibly even as one of the defining features of the bourgeoisie.

Mrs Jean-Baptiste D., for example, rejecting during the course of our interview the supposed equation between bourgeoisie and capital, summed up by insisting on what constitutes the true privilege of people like herself:

Education and a certain quality of ease. For example, every year my grandfather rented a villa in Brittany where we all foregathered. We had the big house at Fontainebleau where we spent every weekend. Those are the real privileges.

Nearly every weekend Mr Georges H. junior, his wife, and their two daughters move out to N., a village lying 40 kilometres outside Paris. There at the family seat the parents work or relax while their daughters enjoy contact with their grandparents, uncles and aunts, and cousins of both sexes. Mr Georges H. junior even does the shopping there at the supermarket and at neighbourhood farms, thus saving time, energy and money, as he points out with a touch of humour.

Mr Pierre I. senior spent every holiday as a boy at his grandfather's house in Béarn as well as at his great-uncles' and great-aunts' houses: 'It was one long party: tennis, volleyball, walks, rambles, swimming in the pool. It was all so easy.' The family still owns those properties, but Mr Pierre I. has preferred to 'concentrate' on his wife's family château. It is close to Paris, so his children and grandchildren can reach it easily, as can friends and more distant relatives.

Tennis, volleyball, walking, riding, and other outdoor activities are inseparably associated with these regular weekends. Exercising the body, tiring it out, combating idleness and softness draw on a certain tradition of physical exertion. In this context one thinks inevitably of the influence of English high society on the customs of the French bourgeoisie from the late nineteenth century onwards. One minor consequence of this (identifiable by ethnographic observation) is that the physical appearance of members of the bourgeoisie bears the stamp of these weekends or brief holidays spent at their country houses. Tanned (or at least pink-cheeked), restored (or at any rate rested), they seem able, thanks to the internal organisation of their family and social life, to escape some of the ravages of 'man's segregation from his natural environment', a segregation that according to Claude Lévi-Strauss constitutes 'a major threat to the mental health of the species' (Lévi-Strauss 1973). The existence of family seats places the bourgeois at the opposite pole from the migrant. His urban way of life is not made up of wrenching breaks or splits. He knows nothing of the exploded kindred, the separation of the generations, weekends spent in the grey monotony of Paris or the suburbs, with the children entrusted to their schools' outdoor centres. His variety of moorings gives him command of his space, and he is not condemned to being deprived of 'nature'.

But the bourgeoisie, you will object, accounts for little of the great flux clogging the ring roads and motorways on Friday and again on Sunday evenings. Granted, but then its migrations bear no resemblance to the practices associated with the second homes of the lower middle classes, practices that are burdened by the often time-consuming processes and sacrifices involved in travelling to and fro. For the bourgeois, the antiquity of the properties, the mixing of the generations, the fact of having roots in the place, mutual assistance among members of the kindred and a certain skill in the practical management of things make such weekends a special time of relaxation bordering on real luxury (not that we should be tempted to underestimate the tensions and individual constraints that go hand in hand with the way such a tribal way of life operates).

The burdens of collective habits, increasing numbers of heirs, shrinking patrimonies, and financial worries hang heavy over the future of such houses. The generation in its fifties is not sure that it will be taking over. Faced with the fear of seeing its family seats disappear, the younger generation, for whom the reality of everyday experience is much like that of the middle classes, is now seeing them for what they are, namely one of its privileges, and not the least of them at that.

These family seats, which have now shed the stigma of social mimicry ('building like their betters'), operate as a crucial distinguishing feature. It is indeed a question of life-style. And that life-style, as Bourdieu points out, is more than just a matter of décor:

Life-style is the first and possibly, today, the most fundamental of these symbolic manifestations, clothing, furnishing, or any other property that, operating according to the logic of belonging and exclusion, reveals differences of capital (understood as capacity to appropriate rare goods and associated benefits) in such a form that they escape the unjustifiable brutality of the fact, *datum brutum*, mere insignificance or pure violence, to attain the misunderstood and desired form of violence (and hence affirmed and recognised as legitimate) that is symbolic violence. (Bourdieu 1978)

Mere insignificances or pure violences, these family seats separate the members of the bourgeois younger generation from their social 'inferiors', the middle classes. In these houses surrounded by ancient orchards, neglected kitchen gardens, and conservatories where 'old Adrien' is no longer to be found tending his tulips, the grandchildren, the last-born, those who attend the state nursery school, are learning to feel abundantly privileged. With the tennis court nearby, the very air they breathe carries an antiquity that breeds distinction.

Let us complete this etymological link between the bourgeois and the town (which by way of a detour through the countryside has given us a glimpse of

8 The 'green elysiums' of childhood

The bourgeois are to some extent able to escape the damaging effects of man's segregation from his natural environment.

the complexity of its treatment) with one further remark. Virtually every historical study of the bourgeoisie of the towns and cities of France has come up against the problem of defining the bourgeois. Duby is just one of many historians to have stated that from as early as the eleventh century the bourgeois has defied all social labelling. The fact that historians have found it so hard to define this individual 'socially', that is to say to make the word match the social reality they are analysing, emphatically heralds the second element that characterises all the definitions.

## The impossibility of categorisation

### The problem of fixing on a moving target

'The word is subject to a host of variations', 'nowadays the meaning of the word is vague and general' – nothing but paradoxes from sources that we expect to set out

the attributes that distinguish a thing, that belong to it to the exclusion of all others. In geometry we recognise only those definitions that logicians call name definitions, that is to say only the giving of names to things that have been clearly designated in terms that are wholly familiar. (*Littré* dictionary)

Are we to conclude that the peculiar characteristics of the bourgeoisie are its diversity, its mobility, its variability in time and space, and for that very reason the impossibility of putting a name to it – in short, its sociological invisibility?

This is the drift of Gay's comments when he talks about historians' 'worried determination' to define the nineteenth-century bourgeoisie (Gay 1984) or Darnton's when he says: 'Historians at all levels of research have responded to the command, find the bourgeois, but have failed to do so' (Darnton 1985). In his detailed study of the public life and political ideas and actions of the French bourgeoisie between 1604 and 1661, Normand confirms the complexity of this elusive social world:

It is a social organism, presented separately in order to appear in its full light, in its curious complication of ranks, dignities, precedences, traditions, rights (of varying degrees of disputedness), pretensions (of varying degrees of legitimacy), and last but by no means least aspirations and desires that have less to do with individuals than with the special milieu in which they move. (Normand 1908)

Whether their chronological reference points are between 1425 and 1450 or the first ten years of the reign of Louis-Philippe [1830–40], all historical studies agree on the mobility of bourgeois society or invite the reader to think of it as 'an expanding milieu' (Daumart 1970). The same author speaks in a more recent work of the fluidity of the bourgeois as 'a group that cannot be defined *a priori* except by accepting what is essentially an unproven and unprovable postulate' (Daumart 1987).

So it is that, from the *Trévoux* to the *Lexis*, the new elements entering into the dictionary definitions relate purely to the evolution of the French economy and French society.

In 1791 the bourgeois was a person belonging to the Third Estate while at the same time being distinguished therefrom by the power of certain privileges. The 1858 *Bescherelle* states:

In general, *bourgeois* is used nowadays to refer to people who live without doing anything, who consume without producing, and whom it is not unusual to see ending their useless existence by being a charge upon society, which has received no service from them.

The term *bourgeoisie*, on the other hand, is defined by the diversity of its acceptations:

– It is used as a collective term and signifies the bourgeois in general, the body of the bourgeois, which includes merchants, well-to-do artisans, shopkeepers, artists, people of private means, lawyers, tax farmers, etc. The bourgeoisie made representations. To marry into the bourgeoisie.
– Sometimes taken for a kind of contempt. Although there is no longer either nobility or clergy, it is almost a disgrace to be of the bourgeoisie.

The 1867 *Larousse* made the bourgeois:

a person of the middle class, that is to say somewhere between the working class and the noble class. The word is often taken in good or ill part according to whether the bourgeois is being compared to the lower class or to the upper class. If the financier misses his mark, the courtiers say of him: 'He's a bourgeois, a nothing man, an oaf; if he is successful, they are after his daughter's hand in marriage' (La Bruyère).

Subsequent encyclopaedic development tried to give an account of the diversity of meanings and usages of the word *bourgeois* (innumerable distinctions between upper and lower, king's bourgeois or itinerant bourgeois, enfeoffed bourgeois, river bourgeois, commonage bourgeois, and 'various other kinds of bourgeois created by local custom'). In conclusion we read: 'It is since 1789 that they have disappeared (nobles and privileged persons), in law at least, for in fact they will always exist. Since then the word bourgeois has been used *in a vague and general way*.'

The *Robert* dictionary puts forward two distinct elements to characterise the bourgeoisie. In the first place the bourgeois is presented as 'a person who does not practise a manual occupation and who usually has a well-paid job'. Secondly, whether or not a person belongs to the bourgeoisie may be judged by his or her 'way of life, intellectual stance, and education'. However, the quotation from the novelist and polemicist Georges Bernanos that punctuates this attempt at a sociological definition once again conveys a pejorative image of the bourgeois: 'the petty bourgeois ... depends wholly on the established order, the established order that he loves as he does himself, for that establishment is his own'. The nineteenth-century *Larousse* takes up this same dual perspective (level of wealth and way of life), though it adds that 'the bourgeois is opposed to the proletarian, and the peasant remains beyond classification for the moment'. The *Lexis* dictionary is the only one to give an account of the Marxist legacy (the bourgeois class owns the means of production), specifying, however, that this trait applies only to capitalist society:

Social class that emerged in Europe during the Middle Ages and that in a capitalist society owns the means of production; by extension, social class comprising those who do not practise a manual occupation and who enjoy a relatively high income or salary.
    'When the dying bourgeoisie shall hear the pavement crack beneath its every step' (Zola).

There follows an extension of the definition that is comparable in every way to the one given by *Larousse* and *Robert*. The emphasis, then, is on the diversity of this social class (upper, middle and lower).

If to these internal distinctions we add the inexactitudes revealed by such expressions as 'the bourgeois is one who makes a *fairly ample* living' or 'one who lives *in some style*', we have to concede the extreme looseness of the definitions put forward as soon as it is a question of pinning down the economic functions and chief social attributes of the bourgeois. 'Bourgeois is today different from commoner in that it conveys an idea of affluence on the part of the person so designated' (*Bescherelle*).

Pure language dictionaries can only, at best, point to 'the most recent meaning', whence their constant use of the expression 'today, bourgeois means ...'. Yesterday it was something different. And tomorrow?

Terminating the discussion in a way, Roland Barthes states: 'The bourgeoisie may be defined as the social class that does not wish to be named' (Barthes 1970). This phenomenon, which Barthes calles 'name defection',[2] should be understood not as a deliberate choice by the bourgeoisie not to be named but as a logical consequence of the process by which this social group is constituted. Down the centuries, the prerequisites for being bourgeois have successively given priority to disparate attributes: man about town, wealthy merchant, industrialist, person of private means, capitalist, family man, and so on. One figure replaces another as the models chop and change. The act of naming or designating ordinarily implies that individuals can be found and recognised within a given social space. The bourgeoisie, however, cannot help but elude this process of categorisation. The only way the status of bourgeois can be understood is in motion.

The first concern of historians who, to pin the bourgeoisie down, seek to

---

[2] Speaking of the phenomenon of name defection, Barthes analyses bourgeois 'ideology' as 'the impulse by which the bourgeoisie turns the reality of the world into an image of the World, History in Nature' (B.L.W.).

immobilise it at a given moment in time is to strip it of its generic name. This is how Braudel writes of the bourgeoisie in the sixteenth century:

In the vocabulary of historians this class or category calls for a word or an expression that easily marks it out in the succession of social forms between the beginning of the reign of François I and the early years of the reign of Louis XIV. If you do not wish to say *Gentry*, neither will you say *upper bourgeoisie*.

This is an allusion to the work of Huppert, an American historian who does indeed use the term *gentry* to describe the men who quit their condition as bourgeois merchants in the towns and cities of France to 'live nobly' (Huppert 1983). To take another example, for a brief period between 1815 and 1848 wealth, family and knowledge came to define a type of private individual, a provincial bourgeois enjoying local power whom historians dubbed a 'notable' (Jardin and Tudescq 1973). This debate about the right word to describe the bourgeois of 1180 or of 1815 is no game of hair-splitting academics. It expresses a genuine feeling of discomfort about putting a name to a social group whose distinguishing feature is its mobility. Mobility is acceptable so long as it remains a matter of an individual or even a family (one might say, for example, that the Xs rose on the social scale) but is intolerable when it comes to characterise a group. However, the bourgeoisie is mobile and for that very reason ever changing and heterogeneous. Depending on time and place, the members who make it up may fulfil different functions. What they will have in common is their ability to move around in social space, preserving the achievements of preceding generations.

## Not a bourgeoisie but bourgeois destinies

Every genealogical account bears witness to this mobility, even if it is partially obscured by the narrative process. Indeed, the genealogical principle (the placing of the generations in order of succession) itself obeys a logic that generates an illusion of continuity.

*The Laure C. family: an old, unchallenged upper bourgeoisie* The history of the Laure C. family, which belongs to the industrial *haute bourgeoisie*, ties in so closely with the history of France that it is impossible to talk about one without coming across the other. It offers a fine example of mobility (understood as the ability to traverse social space without necessarily changing status), revealing how it becomes impossible to group all these women and all these men under a single label. The C. family emerged from obscure origins in Lorraine in 1704, when they purchased an old ruined forge in the Moellan Basin. Seven generations ensued, covering a quarter of a millennium and ensuring continuity. To begin with, we are told by the historian of the C.s (mention of whose name would betray the identity of the family) that they were soldiers and minor law officers and intendants of the camps and armies of the King; there was also a President-General of the Salt Excise and a President at the Office of Finance. Then came the national professional colleges [*grandes écoles*]: the Ecole des Mines, the Ecole Centrale, and the Ecole polytechnique. Lastly there were seats on the major national assemblies: the Departmental Council [*conseil général*] of Moselle, the Chamber of Deputies, the Senate, the Academy, the Council of Administrators [*conseil des régents*] of the Bank of France, and so on. The author concludes: 'For some two centuries they surmounted many obstacles ... In their very trials they tempered their resolution.'

The heir to this history, Mrs Laure C. senior, sums it up in broad brush-strokes, stressing the moral values handed down through this vast family.

My mother's family were modern in their approach. They were a clan. Everything was in exclusively family hands. There were three brothers and my father, who had been as it were co-opted to manage part of the firm (an industrial empire). Each of them had his residences, his interests, his shares. It was an industrious as well as an industrial company, austere, with the accent on work. It would have been unacceptable for them each not to set themselves work targets. My maternal grandmother played an enormous role, interested in the major social problems of her day (training of nurses and female schoolteachers). By contrast, in my father's family my grandfather and his first cousin did not live from any paid work. The atmosphere was different there. It was a family in which one lived on one's private income, a gentler, more traditional sort of family. They all got together somewhere near the Paris region during the holidays. The two sides knew each other but did not have the same tastes, their view of the world was different. Neither the same interests, nor the same tastes. And yet my father's family were very well-to-do, they had been extremely wealthy in the eighteenth and nineteenth centuries: Eastern textiles, bankers, big industrialists. They had married into the banks that financed much of our industrial development. Their children had taken no interest in business.

Mrs Laure C. senior currently resides in the sixteenth district. A top civil servant, she is the widow of an international lawyer who himself came of an ancient bourgeois and noble family from northern France. A family history was written in connection with him. Covering twenty generations, it is prefaced by this quotation from the novelist and critic Paul Bourget: 'The individual is but a moment in his race.' Everything recommences with each generation, hence the diversity and the inevitable mobility. To illustrate this in concrete terms, let us look at a few remarks gathered from the mouths of three generations of women in the Laure C. family, remarks concerning the social positions of a certain number of their relatives.

Mrs Laure C. senior has a sister who is married to the head of a radio network; the couple have a son of school age and live in Paris, in the fifth district. Another brother took over the parts of the family empire that had not been nationalised; married and with small children, he lives in an *hôtel particulier* in the historic Marais quarter of Paris. The informant has another sister, who is married to the chairman of a large textile company. The couple have two daughters, one an English teacher and the other a self-styled 'adventuress'. Of their three sons, one owns ready-to-wear clothing shops and is married to 'a woman from a paper-industry family'; they live in the sixteenth district. A second son is a film producer; the third is reading for a political-science degree.

Mrs Laure C. senior has three aunts on her mother's side. One is married to a retired inspector of taxes 'descended from a noble family'. They live in the sixteenth district. She does not know what her children do, though she sees them three times a year. Their grandmother supplies certain details: the couple have two daughters and a son; one of the daughters is married 'to an *énarque* [a student or graduate of the Ecole nationale d'administration]' and the other to an aristocrat who 'is in business, a personnel manager', while the son is a literary critic. Mrs Laure C. senior's second aunt died from the effects of her imprisonment during the Second World War. 'She was in the Resistance.' The third aunt is married to Count X, another tax inspector and one of the people who manage the family's affairs. The couple reside in the sixth district and have two children. The son manages an industrial concern and lives in the same street as his parents. The daughter is married to Marquis X, a landowner, and they in turn have a daughter, 'the brains of the family'.

Finally, Mrs Laure C. senior has a paternal aunt who is the widow of a count, a former member of the Academy of Moral and Political Sciences and a collector. She lives in an *hôtel particulier* in the eighth district on the income from her estates.

The informant spoke in detail about her maternal great-uncles and great-aunts and their descendants. One great-uncle, now deceased, had never married and had once managed the industrial empire; another, who died a quarter of a century ago, had been a manager at the Bank of France and a senator. This great-uncle had had a daughter, who married her first cousin, 'the real boss of the empire'. The couple had eight children, the sons becoming industrialists and the daughters psychiatrists or marrying ministers of the Fifth Republic. Two other children of this great-uncle married 'into the upper aristocracy', and Laure C. junior is in touch with her cousins of both sexes. One is a sculptress, she told me, another looks after the estate, another is married to 'a double-barrelled name', and there are also an anthropologist, a commercial executive and an illustrator 'married to an aristocrat'.

These informants also supplied detailed information concerning the occupations and marriages of the descendants of their paternal great-uncles and great-aunts. The paternal side of the family forged numerous alliances with the landed aristocracy. Certain descendants still live on the income from their estates, others are chairmen of big businesses, managing directors of companies, and engineers 'married to countesses'.

The diversity of occupations cited does not rule out certain limits. As specified by the *Robert* and *Larousse* dictionaries, manual occupations are absent. In the mouths of my informants, occupation and quality of marriage were placed on the same level. This family presents all the characteristics of the industrial upper bourgeoisie that over the space of two centuries has been marrying into the landed aristocracy.

*A confident, easy-going bourgeoisie* Sandrine, aged 32, talked about her family's origins in very technical terms, without the details or anecdotes that would have made it more of a narrative. She simply listed the social functions occupied by some of the men of her family. The fact of belonging to the bourgeoisie was taken for granted.

My father did law, he was a solicitor, then a barrister. His father was an industrialist, a colonel, a member of the Resistance, shot in '44. My great-grandfather was chief of the Paris police. My mother's father was from an entirely similar family, the Ys. My father and mother met in the Midi through great-uncles.

Sandrine's mother's family had been provincial solicitors for several generations.

The fragments of her autobiography that were thrown up at random during the course of an interview that turned into a conversation bear witness to the extraordinary continuity of the bourgeois condition, a continuity that is experienced as something natural. Sandrine met her husband at a ball at the age of 16. They met again some years later and got married when Sandrine was 27. They have two children. Sandrine works part-time (assistant curator in a museum), 'not for financial reasons but for pleasure', she says. Her husband is an auditor, a partner in a firm. His mother gave them an apartment in the seventh district. 'My husband's family is aristocratic, but from the point of view of education there's nothing in it.'

On the walls hang ancestral portraits, together with a number of oil-paintings and watercolours. Set out on a chest of drawers in the drawing-room is the family silver. The telephone rings and Sandrine answers it (it transpires that she addresses her mother as *vous*): she has to get ready to go and fetch her sister and leave for B. to spend the weekend at the family seat. Her husband will join her later that evening. The weather is so warm. Sandrine is expecting her second child and the first needs to play, needs a chance to run about with the cousins. It is all perfectly natural, taken for granted.

*A classic bourgeoisie* Christiane supplied few details; everything in her account was self-evident:

My father was a director of the Bank of France; his family is from the Vendée originally. They are soldiers, sailors, solicitors, lawyers. Grandfather came to Paris and started an insurance company. My mother's family were solicitors for four or five generations. They were a wealthy family, a bourgeois mafia, where everything was handed down, but on the whole things went all right.

Two of Christiane's brothers are soldiers. One is married to 'a girl from the Reims bourgeoisie, a second or third cousin'. A third brother, an auctioneer (the practice was bought with the maternal family's money), is about to marry a young woman 'belonging to the old Vendée nobility. They met at the family seat; she is a very devout Catholic – it's a family that lives off its estates.' Christiane, a 'psychomotrician' with two children, is married to a product manager from 'a bourgeois family but one with no descent', she states specifically.

## One is always somebody's bourgeois

Mobility, diversity: in short, everybody is bourgeois in someone's eyes – starting with the cabbie or the workman when they call 'bourgeois' all the people whom they serve.

– Said by workmen of the people for whom they work, regardless of their quality. To work for the bourgeois. One must not deceive the bourgeois.
– Servants and working men and women of the various trades refer in this way to the master or mistress who employs them. Our bourgeois. His bourgeois is not happy. His bourgeoise has sacked him.
– Appellation also used by cab drivers and coachmen when speaking of the person or persons they have driven somewhere.
Where do you want to go, bourgeois? I drove this bourgeois to the Place Royale (*Bescherelle*).

Clearly, working-class usages of the word *bourgeois* spring from a simple concept of otherness: anyone a worker served would be called 'bourgeois'. Such practices, now possibly obsolete, nevertheless prompt one to ask what conception the bourgeois has of otherness.

Firstly, there are the 'radically other' – foreigners, working people, sometimes Jews, people one does not know, people whose very way of life one knows nothing about.

We were completely ignorant of how people lived who were not like us. We had no contact, as children, with working-class children. (Mrs Laure C. senior)

For Mrs Emilie E., Jews and workers were strangers: 'It's possibly wrong of me to say that because my children have married Jews, but in our milieu we didn't know what that was. I find it absurd, but that was the case.' The same person said that the first time she saw a worker was when she went into the provinces with her husband's firm. Certain historical events brought about the encounter. Such was the part played by the First World War in the life of Mrs Arnold A. She took a job as a waitress in a canteen frequented by working men's wives. 'I did not know them at all. We only saw country people. I felt a tremendous gulf, discovering those women, in fact I still feel it.'

The generations brought up before the war were aware of this isolation and deplored it.

One never even saw one's friends from Sainte Marie again because they didn't belong to the same milieu. One would have liked to go to school without a chauffeur and without a chaperon, like the others. One wanted to follow R. Garric.[3] (Mrs Laure C. senior's mother)

Nowadays the younger generation claims to 'mix with all sorts' [*fréquenter tous les milieux*]. The foundations of their education remain the same, however, and we shall see how Sainte Marie girls, for example, feel just as much prisoners of their world today as did their grandmothers.

At the time, people associated hideous practices with other social milieux, sometimes as part of a deliberate rebellion. Take Simone de Beauvoir:

Workmen in particular belonged to a species that was as dangerously alien as the Boches or the Bolsheviks ... I was especially pleased when I chanced to come into contact with some working-class people ... And I used to think of that man, R. Garric, who was different from everyone else and who lived in an unfamiliar, almost exotic quarter [of Paris]: Belleville. (Beauvoir 1958)

Belleville was the very place where Laure C. junior lived after her marriage. Twelve years later she moved to Neuilly:

Neuilly was fascinating, it was like landing in cotton wool. People smiled, women took their children for walks. Was this normal? In Belleville I had forgotten this kind of civility. I thank heaven that I did live there for a few years. Coming from an over-protected milieu, I was able to take on board the fact that life is sometimes hard.

For the granddaughter, in effect, the grandmother's wish had come true.

Matching this vision of a remote Other, there is the vision of an Other who is close. It is through observing their internal diversity that members of the bourgeoisie conceive this far from remote otherness, the kind that generates the illusion of 'mixing with all sorts'. People will always find someone rather more or rather less bourgeois than themselves or almost equally so. Through being exposed and consciously identified, these differences function as distinguishing criteria; they also serve to assign individuals to the places that are strictly theirs.

'We were friends with the Xs, a family in the limelight at the same time as ourselves' (Mrs Arnold A.). 'We were a little more affluent than the milieu described by Simone de Beauvoir' (Mrs Emile E.) 'I didn't go to balls. There was far more money in industrial circles than in the magistracy. In our day we were poor. We were limited by father's salary. The magistracy lived more on moral prestige than on money' (Mr Charles B.).

There are some bourgeois who have no conception of other people. I'm talking about a tiny fringe of the bourgeoisie, the people who frequent the Automobile Club. They're pretentious. There's also an impecunious bourgeoisie, infinitely deserving, who often

---

[3] R. Garric was a prominent figure in the Catholic religious revival that followed the First World War. Convinced that faith and reason (social Catholicism and the 'intellectual élites') could go hand in hand, he founded the *Equipes sociales* with the object of reconciling the social classes in France. See also the Simone de Beauvoir quotation below.

9 *Pièces rapportées* ['new blood']
Daughters-in-law and sisters-in-law are obliged, for instance, to show a certain reserve.

have lots of children, no money, and few country houses or none at all because the other branch hung on to them. (Mrs Pierre I. senior).

Mr Georges H. junior presents himself as 'the man who has a bit less of everything, a bit less status, a bit less of the ready'. Speaking of one of his cousins, he declares: 'He's a true bourgeois, that one. He had a logical career, not brilliant but logical. He didn't go poking his nose in elsewhere.'

This view of the close Other literally puts people and things into order. It fulfils a comparable function to that described by Augé in connection with lineal societies, where the conception of otherness is

a game on the frontiers that tends either to assimilate the other and relaunch the internal dynamic of difference or to expel the other in order to stake out the limits of identity (for instance, abominable and unnatural practices are attributed to foreigners, who are regarded as absolutely other). (Augé 1987)

As regards the first tendency, take the expression *pièce rapportée*,[4] which is in everyday use in bourgeois families. It generally denotes daughter-in-law (when used by parents) or sister-in-law (when used by brothers). In practical terms it presupposes a large phratry. In using the phrase the group is indicating in an immensely kind way the 'familiar strangeness' of its relations

---

4 Borrowed, in this instance, from dressmaking, a *pièce rapportée* being a piece of contrasting material added to, say, a dress. The figurative sense invoked is something like 'new blood'.

by marriage. Daughters-in-law and sisters-in-law are obliged, for instance, to show a certain reserve, observe a certain discretion. It is hardly the done thing, for example, for a *pièce rapportée* to mention in public the authoritarian manner of the female head of the family or to comment on the way things are run. In such ways blood relations remind their relations by marriage that they have been 'introduced'. Hence the role of those private jokes or quotations that circulate among the members of the group like so many passwords that must remain incomprehensible to the *pièce rapportée*. By isolating this very close Other in her singularity, the group preserves the identity that the marriage has inevitably 'jangled'. It should be added that daughters-in-law and sisters-in-law are in no way alarmed by this game. Coming from 'almost identical' circles, they have often been and will often be on the other side of the situation. Indeed, the expression *pièces rapportées* is not used in connection with misalliances. In such cases there is no question of 'introducing' anyone, unless the mother chooses to show humanity. The private jokes would then lose their charm, being only too trivially true.

Alternatively, the Other is expelled. Two ways of achieving this are commonly employed. The first is (dare one say it?) a plain social fact: people do not in fact frequent all milieux, even where they harbour the illusion of doing so. The second comes down to working out subtle degrees of proximity. Friends who come from an 'elsewhere' that, though close, is regarded as too remote will not be invited to visit the family seat. Other friends will on the contrary be introduced to the group straight away.

This delicate game of frontiers (which supplied much of the subject-matter of our conversations) presupposes a permanent process of reflection on the regulation of relationships with other people. This is how the bourgeoisie lives off its own diversity, by ceaselessly drawing on it to renew itself.

In the dictionary definitions this diversity is clearly indicated by the word's multiplicity of acceptations. It reveals a mobility that may be understood as the ability on the part of a particular social group to make the most appropriate choices in order to sustain and develop the acquisitions of previous generations. If we accept what Touraine says, this is one of the essential features of a ruling class:

A social class is defined as ruling not on the basis of its economic integration but by its ability to shift and then control the things that are at issue in social relations, in short by its aim to control the historicity of a society. (Touraine, quoted by Bidou *et al.* 1983)

Diversity may also relate to heterogeneity. To postulate this assertion is to make it impossible to use the term *bourgeois*, let alone set out to study 'the bourgeoisie' in general. We find ourselves back in the imbroglio we started with: employing the generic term 'bourgeoisie' arouses the irritable suscepti-bilities of those who form part of it and inevitably brings one back to the naïve subjectivity of those who speak of it thus.

So the words *bourgeois/bourgeoisie* denote a shifting reality. However, this characteristic, which has to be seen as belonging peculiarly to the thing referred to, cannot take the place of an explanation of the taboo affecting the use of these words.

## The emergence of a culture

The double negative, specific uses of *bourgeois* as an adjective, and derogatory use are the last three elements characterising the definitions. It is in analysing them together (even if for the sake of convenience of exposition we have to deal with the problem of the double negative separately) that we see the existence of a bourgeois culture emerge in a jumble of meanings.

The blurred frontiers between the permanent elements of the meanings of words and their subjective values here give rise to a denial of which we need to trace the logical consequences.

For example (and the example chosen is the most topical), what meaning is one to give to the implied connection between the 'affluent social position' of the bourgeois (a vague but consistent feature of the definitions) and 'the cult of the material self' of which the bourgeois is said to be a follower?

Borrowing Sahlins' anthropological critique of the conception of human cultures that 'are worked out on the basis of practical activity and utilitarian interest' (Sahlins 1980), we get:

Bourgeoisie = class producing material goods = absence of spirituality.

Bourgeois = owner of assets, horizontal being = lacking verticality.

It is an act of denial making the bourgeois a being without culture, a person for whom all access to the symbolic is organically impossible. This correlation, reducing social order to the level of praxis, is surely too much of a caricature for us not to be tempted to look for its foundations and identify the factors on which it hinges.

### *The double negative: neither . . . nor . . .*

'Neither nobleman nor soldier, neither peasant nor worker, such is the bourgeois.' A double negative thus defines the bourgeoisie as an in-between or middle class. *Trévoux* speaks of a class mid-way between nobility and peasantry. The nineteenth-century *Larousse* talks about a person of the middle class, that is to say 'between the working class and the noble class'. The twentieth-century *Larousse* echoes the same wording: 'nowadays – person of the middle class – mid-way between people and nobility, hence a non-noble person'. *Lexis* drops the contrast with nobility to detail the internal distinctions peculiar to the bourgeoisie.

In indicating a position, the notion of a middle class denotes a tract of social terrain with ill-defined outlines. The expression would certainly not be

adequate today to furnish a social and cultural definition of the 'old'
bourgeoisie. On the other hand, in terms of a social ethic and taking only the
adjective 'middle' [*moyen*], it is possible to identify certain features specific to
bourgeois culture. The happy medium, in-betweenness, and the anti-hero
were positions claimed by the French bourgeoisie very early on. We need look
no further than the address to the reader in Antoine Furetière's *Roman
bourgeois* [literally 'bourgeois novel'], published in 1666, where the author
defines the type of his novel as being opposed to those of the epic or the poetic
fiction. He has no desire, he says, to 'start at the wrong end'. He wishes to
recount

sincerely and faithfully certain anecdotes or love stories occurring between persons
who will be neither heroes nor heroines and will draw up no armies and conquer no
kingdoms but who will be among those good people of the middle rank who quietly
pursue their destinies, some of them good-looking, others ugly, some wise, others
foolish; and the latter look very much as if they make up the great majority. (Furetière
1981)

'Middle' in the definitions is defined by two extremes: the Great and the
Poor. The nobility casts a belittling shadow over the bourgeoisie whilst the
poor man throws back the shadow of a 'shameful' (because illegitimate)
domination. The nineteenth century may have formalised and fixed the
caricature of the bourgeois, but it did not create it. We need to let history put
things in perspective.

It was in the eleventh century, Duby tells us, that the question first arose as to
where to place these folk who lived in towns and could not be lumped
together with poor and peasants. They did not fit into the triangular figure
that was the ideal representation of the social order.

They [townspeople] were stationed at the springs of the new posterity, the one fostered
by the growing vigour of monetary circuits ... Where should they be placed? What
word could be found to describe these people?[5] ... Eventually, towards the end of the
eleventh century, at the time of the First Crusade, the people who drew up charters
inserted into the lists of witnesses, between the groups of knights and peasants,
dominated by the former, overlooking the latter, the group of 'bourgeois and
sergeants'. *Notice that these two terms would have had no functional connotation* ... That
should not surprise us, for the belated, furtive emergence of this category in written
form on documents whose role was to establish rights was oddly disturbing. There
were indeed several ways in which it clouded the view that those capable of reflective
thought traditionally took of the social order. Putting the 'bourgeois' in a separate
category meant admitting that the countryside was not everything, that there existed
a different social space with its own particular structure, the urban milieu, that it
contained specialists of the third function [i.e. 'workers', as distinct from clergy and
nobles] but who did not fulfil that function in quite the same way [i.e. as the *laboureur*

---

5   The problem of naming (which is where we started) is thus the same as that of where to place
    'these people' called 'bourgeois'. Remember, the etymological sense cannot correspond to the
    whole of the reality referred to (B. L. W.).

or farmer], a fact that had to be taken into account in any analysis of society in functional terms. (Duby 1978)

However, things did not go entirely smoothly, thirty or forty generations in succession having represented social perfection to themselves in the form of tri-functionality. 'This mental picture had withstood all the pressures of history. It was a structure' (*ibid.*).

The institution of the monarchical state has room for the clergy, the nobility, and, according to Richet, 'a negative order defined only by what it was excluded from: not privilege, certainly, but blue blood and the service of God' (Richet 1969). The syntactical form of the double negative used in the definitions is testimony to the liveliness of this 'negative' conception of the bourgeoisie.

On the eve of the French Revolution this fourth order (a disruptive element in terms of the ideal organisation of society) set out to win its place. That meant first of all establishing itself in the Christian scheme of things, which organised the social order between the Great and the Poor.

God created the Rich Man in order that he might ransom his sins by succouring the poor; he created the Poor Man in order that he might be humbled by the help he receives from the Rich Man . . . Thus in Christian legend great and poor will each have claims to assert. But where, on the other hand, are those of the bourgeois? (Groethuysen 1977)

The bourgeois: a being without the guardian angel of class; the bourgeoisie: an essentially secular phenomenon – characteristics that as early as the eleventh century could not help disturbing 'those capable of reflective thought', in Duby's words. 'Would the Church be able to consecrate the bourgeois, would it be able to elevate the bourgeoisie to the dignity of a religious symbol?' (*ibid*).

Groethuysen's work recounts the various stages of the conflict between the bourgeoisie and the Church. The bourgeoisie sought to destroy an ideal conception of the social order from which it was excluded. The first thing was to get rid of the Poor Man by depriving him of his transcendental character and suggesting that everyone become 'bourgeois'. This is why 'no one can blame you for not being a duke or a marquis, but it is always rather your fault if you are not in a condition of bourgeoisie'. The bourgeois wants to be judged on his everyday existence, which is made up of honest affluence and reasoned foresight, with work becoming a virtue. On this point the bourgeoisie was to find preachers to suit it. On the other hand it was to clash with the Church when the latter taught humility while the former was trying to better itself. 'The ambitious upset the social order, ambition carries us to a rank to which we ought not to aspire since it is above our condition', said the seventeenth-century Jesuit preacher Louis Bourdaloue, whom Groethuysen quotes.

The good man will be moral without the advice of the Church.

The bourgeoisie had created for itself a fresh conception of life; to make that conception prevail it presented it in general terms and elevated it to a world order ... It was its own existence that was to furnish its supreme argument, and in opposition to the pious souls who spoke of the vanity of human effort in the face of death, the bourgeois believed in life and was successful. (*ibid.*)

The bourgeoisie was natural; it did not emanate from divine power. So it was able to offer its ethic as universal. However, it soon bowed to reason, accepting that it is not given to everyone to be a good man.

'For the lower classes, everything was to remain as in the past: they must continue to believe. No one must entertain any illusions on the subject, Necker tells us in his book on The Importance of Religious Opinions' (*ibid.*). But in putting forward its cultural order as universal, the bourgeoisie at the same time made it impossible for it to call itself a privileged part of French society.

This is also how

bourgeois ideology is thus able to fill everything and without risk lose its name in it: no one, there, will return it; it is able without resistance to subsume the theatre, art, bourgeois man under their eternal analogues; in a word, it is able to ex-name itself without restriction when there is no longer anything but one and the same human nature: here bourgeois name defection is complete. (Barthes 1970)

The bourgeoisie is in constant movement, and in that movement it eludes all categorisation, clashing head-on with an ideal conception of the social order without being capable of supplying a different one. Its claim to universality (supposed mobility of individuals within social relationships) was to be demolished all through the nineteenth century by socialist movements and Marxist theorists.

In the symbolism of the Nation State the bourgeoisie was scarcely represented. The fourth order found no place.

Every society must invent and imagine the legitimacy it grants to power ... Indeed, no culture and hence no power may be deduced from any universal physical, biological, or spiritual principle, not being bound by any kind of internal relationship to the 'nature of things' or to 'human nature'. (Baczko 1984)

This symbolic absence at the level of political representation needs to be related to the denial by French society of the existence of a bourgeois culture. The ultimate complexity is that the bourgeoisie participates in that denial (bourgeois writers disowning their origins in order to be recognised and to acknowledge themselves as creators). And yet production, in Sahlins' words, is no more than a 'practical logic of material efficiency' (Sahlins 1980). If such were indeed the case, why do Americans not eat horseflesh?

In the course of his exposition Sahlins cannot help mentioning a specific feature of Western society, namely the way in which it excels in obscuring its symbol production. He speaks of it as being 'forgetful of its own cultural base'.

This explains why he calls one of the chapters of his book: 'Bourgeois thought, Western society: a culture'. By using the adjective 'bourgeois' the author somehow wards off the taboo that Western society casts upon itself when it refuses to acknowledge the existence of a symbolic code in *capitalist* society. The pejorative sense running through all the definitions is simply the expression of that denial.

## As used pejoratively

Brooding – the aesthetic delight of the bourgeoisie. (Jean Giraudoux, *Littérature*)

In the language of the bourgeoisie, the grandeur of the words is in direct proportion to the pettiness of the sentiments. (E. and J. de Goncourt, *Idées et Sensations*)

It is something quite unique to the bourgeoisie, I believe, this cowardice in social relations. By cowardice I mean the talent for consideration and base accommodation that prevents people who detest one another from quarrelling. (E. and J. de Goncourt, *Journal*)

People have made the mistake of trying to turn the bourgeoisie into a class. The bourgeoisie is quite simply the contented portion of the populace. The bourgeois is the man who now has time to sit down. A chair is not a caste. (Victor Hugo, *Les Misérables*)

A bourgeois is the sea of nothingness. (E. and J. de Goncourt, *Journal*)

Duty (with a capital D) was the name the bourgeoisie had given to its moral cowardice. (Valery Larbaud, *A.-O. Barnabooth*)

The virtue of men such as my Uncle Louis is to seek a maximum of approval for a minimum of risks. ('What a splendid definition of the bourgeoisie!' thought Costals). (Henri de Montherlant, *Pitié pour les femmes*)

The horror of the bourgeois is itself bourgeois. (Jules Renard, *Journal*)

'I want,' he [Nizan] had written, 'to fight real men.' He thought of the bourgeois then, but the bourgeois are faceless: the person you think you hate vanishes, and you are left with Standard Oil or the Stock Exchange. (Jean-Paul Sartre, *Situations IV*)

What is a bourgeois? I give you this definition: someone who has reservations. (A. Siegried, *Tableau des partis en France*)

The bourgeois use their daughters to manure the lands of the quality. (de Chamfort)

Let the good bourgeois enjoy their married life: it was for them alone that Hymen instituted permitted pleasures. (La Fontaine)

As we have shown on a number of occasions, from *Trévoux* to *Lexis* the dictionary definitions are coloured by the pejorative sense in an oddly insistent way. Does the same thing happen with the nobleman, the worker or the peasant? It does not, though there is an exception in the case of the peasant [*paysan*]. *Littré* gives: 'pejorative and popular: *bouseux* [yokel], *culterreux* [clodhopper], *pécore* [stupid person], *péquenot* [country bumpkin]; the manners of a peasant: unrefined'. Note that the pejorative sense is associated with popular usage, whereas the popular sense of the word *bourgeois* relates only to the social condition of the speaker: 'It is the cabbie or the workman who call bourgeois anyone whom they serve.'

What elements does denigration target? The whole person of the bourgeois from smell [*cela sent son bourgeois*] to name ('this name does not suggest that the bearer of it is of a particularly lofty station'), taking in ways of moving, speaking, and thinking.

The table on pp. 55–7 sets out the 'as used pejoratively' entries alongside 'specific usages of the adjective bourgeois'.

The pejorative sense gives an impression of the bourgeois as an extremely deprived person. He is mainly 'lacking in ...'. He lacks nobility. 'The bourgeois is not noble: that is in fact one of the definitions of the word', wrote the Duc de Brissac in his introduction to the genealogical compendium of the old bourgeoisie. This question of the bourgeoisie's being subject to the aristocracy verges on the obsessional. It is there already at the level of the analysis of etymological meaning, so we cannot simply brush it aside. Also, to deal with it properly we need to go back to the general history of the bourgeoisie. And that history spans a long period – more than eight centuries, in fact!

In his book on 'the persistence of the Ancien Régime', Mayer puts forward a radical hypothesis: 'The bourgeois did not exert the influence they might have had on the creation of a new aesthetics and a new spirit.' In fact, he writes, they 'helped to sustain and reproduce the cultural system of the Ancien Régime' (Mayer 1983). The bourgeoisie was a willing victim, seeking only to be acknowledged and assimilated by the aristocracy. Mayer's hypothesis is not in conflict with that other theory that a bourgeois culture quietly blossomed that had its roots in the very centuries when in order to exist the bourgeoisie sought to stay out of the limelight. Culture or the formation of a culture does not boil down to a simple accounting process of pluses and minuses. Yet the definitions we have been looking at all reflect this mechanistic concept of the phenomenon.

Nobility is something the bourgeois lacks genetically, hence the way in which the contempt fastens on physical aspects (look, smell, bearing, turns of speech, styles of dress, etc.). From a lack of genetic nobility to a lack of moral nobility is but a step. The bourgeois is a being without stature but also without breadth (of mind).

The distinguishing features of the bourgeois as an individual are thus thought of as a conditioned response to the place the bourgeois occupies in the world of capitalist production (cf. reduction of the symbolic order to praxis).

| As used pejoratively | Specific usages of the adjective *bourgeois(e)* |
|---|---|
| *Trévoux*<br>– 'Used pejoratively to refer to a man who is not a gentleman or who has no breeding', 'you can smell the bourgeois on him'.<br>– 'how utterly bourgeois' [*cela est du dernier bourgeois*].<br>– Low [*basses*] and vulgar [*populaires*]. | – a house: built simply and without splendour but convenient and habitable. As opposed to palace or hotel or hut or peasant's or worker's house.<br>– a family: a family that is not noble but is above artisan level.<br>– manners, turns of speech.<br>– wine: the wine gathered by the bourgeois of Paris, which they are entitled to sell by the jar from their own premises; wine in one's cellar, as opposed to tavern wine.<br>– bourgeois soup: good, ordinary soup. |
| *Bescherelle*<br>– 'Used pejoratively to denigrate or reproach a man either because he is not a gentleman or because he lacks the social graces.'<br>– 'they feel their bourgeois are wealthy and respected'<br>– 'Looking common, having common manners'<br>– 'This name does not suggest that the bearer is of a particularly lofty station.' Bourgeoisie: occasionally taken for a kind of contempt. | – acting: acting purely for one's one amusement.<br>– everyday fare, soup, house: simple and clean, without luxury or affectation.<br>– fish<br>– wine<br>– coat<br>– suit<br>– appearance, manners, name<br>– culinary art: very simple way of preparing food. |
| Nineteenth-century *Larousse*<br>– 'This word is often taken in good part or amiss depending on whether the bourgeois is being compared to the class below or the class above.'<br>– 'The bourgeois is blinkered and vain.'<br>– 'To do the bourgeois thing [*faire le bourgeois*]: to buy a house in the country and withdraw from Parisian life.'<br>– 'The bourgeois will always be an artisan who has made good.'<br>– In denigration, a person who lacks distinction, with only vulgar and common tastes.<br>– 'The bourgeois is someone who is a stranger to any knowledge of or even taste for the fine arts.' | – house: well kept but without luxury.<br>– cooking: dishes of good quality but simple in terms of preparation.<br>– boarding-house: establishment providing bourgeois cooking for a set number of guests.<br>– theatre: show put on by mere amateurs rather than by professionals.<br>– coat: as opposed to a uniform coat.<br>– wine: (cf. *Trévoux*).<br>– fish: the share retained by the owner of the boat.<br>– calf's liver: simple way of preparing a dish, typical of bourgeois cooking. |

| As used pejoratively | Specific usages of the adjective *bourgeois(e)* |
|---|---|
| **Nineteenth) century *Larousse (cont.)*** <br> – 'The bourgeois is someone who practices the cult of the material self', etc. <br> – Without dignity, without nobility, without generosity, mean-minded, vulgar, common, bourgeois virtues, a bourgeois air. <br> – 'That smells of the worst kind of bourgeois' [*Cela sent le bourgeois du plus méchant aloi*] | – bourgeois ways: peculiar to the bourgeois, bourgeois simplicity. |
| **Robert** <br> – Pejorative sense, person lacking both distinction and culture. <br>   Particular pejorative usage: Person of little taste, taking no interest in the arts and literature. | – way of life, intellectual attitude, education, to live, think, or act as a bourgeois. <br> – Backed by derogatory quotations. |

'The true bourgeois is by nature the peaceable and idle owner of what he has; he is always pleased with himself and easily pleased with others' (Joubert, XVI.24).

| | |
|---|---|
| – Bourgeois airs; common, vulgar; ideas, tastes (old-fashioned and excessively conservative). <br><br><br><br><br><br><br><br><br><br> Antonyms: <br> 1) yokel, villein, serf, artisan <br> 2) aristocrat, noble, proletarian worker <br> 3) countryman, peasant, soldier, artist, adventurer, Bohemian. | – Also said of a home-loving person who likes his comfort, settled, stay-at-home. <br> – Bourgeois life, habits, education, childhood, heredity. <br> Special uses: <br> – Cooking: good, plain. <br> – House: as opposed to hotel or mansion. <br> – Acting: drawing-room theatre. <br> – Coat: as opposed to uniform. |
| **Twentieth-century *Larousse*** <br> – 'Person of no distinction who has only common sentiments and vulgar tastes.' <br> – 'Nowadays what is in the nature of an old-fashioned or Prudhommesque[a] conservative: it's so bourgeois . . . what he's telling us there!!!' <br> – 'Who lacks distinction, who always places the material above what is beautiful and refined.' | – Feelings <br> – House: 'where a certain style of life is maintained'. <br> – Boarding-house, cooking, calf's liver, theatre, coat, wine (cf. *Bescherelle* and the others). |

[a] Monsieur Joseph Prudhomme, a creation of the caricaturist Henri Monnier (1799–1877), personified the dull, prosperous bourgeois of the 1830s and 1840s [Tr.].

*An impossible code: cultural self-sufficiency*

By concentrating on the specific uses of the adjective, we begin to see what characteristics are seen as peculiarly bourgeois, characteristics that carry a generally positive connotation. The basic elements of this 'culture' are eminently 'material': a house, a kind of cooking, a kind of theatre, wine, fish, calf's liver, a coat. What do they have in common through being bourgeois?

The house is simple, comfortable without being in any way magnificent. It may be contrasted with the luxury of the mansion as much as with the poverty of the shack (cf. neither . . . nor . . .). It is as if constructed between two representations. (The reader is referred to the works of J.-P. Chalinnes as well as to those analysing the nineteenth-century compendia of architects' examples that echo the changes in bourgeois fashions and life-styles, formalised through the organisation of living-space.)

Bourgeois wine is the kind that the bourgeois of Paris made and drank themselves (as opposed to tavern wine).

Bourgeois theatre is the kind one put on at home for one's own amusement, using amateur actors.

Bourgeois cooking was characterised by simplicity in the preparation of food.

Simplicity, self-sufficiency, neutrality: in short, an advancement of the private sphere as opposed to the public. This 'stereotyped' image of the bourgeoisie matches that formed in the nineteenth century (cf. studies of the nineteenth-century Swedish bourgeoisie).

Today, however (and the twentieth-century *Larousse* bears this out), a bourgeois house means 'a house where a certain style of life is maintained'. So nowadays the adjective *bourgeois* suggests luxury, wealth or privilege. But remember: bourgeois luxury has to be experienced and displayed modestly and humbly. Otherwise one runs the risk of being bracketed with that dreadful species, the upstarts [*les parvenus*]. As Mrs Pierre I. declared vehemently:

At the Automobile Club there are a great many snobs, people who attach too much importance to externals, to grooming. For instance, I'm against mink and all that sort of frippery. Last Sunday we were forty-one at the château. There were some friends from the theatre group [these are friends with whom Mrs Pierre I. organises regular outings to the theatre], they're less wealthy than ourselves. I took care to dress for the country. One shouldn't overwhelm. It's not worth it.

Let us dwell for a moment on the example of bourgeois dress. Through it we can trace the formation and development of a true culture. The history of costume reveals how the bourgeoisie has repeatedly replaced the aristocracy's ostentatious distinguishing marks with marks that are more restrained, more discreet, though no less formidable in terms of symbolic effectiveness.

10  Ear-rings

By studying the bourgeois outfit we are able to trace the formation and development of a genuine culture.

Bourgeois dress stands in contrast to noble dress and to uniform. These two have in common the fact of being visible and immediately identifiable on the social stage. They made it easy to read the station or quality of the wearer.

Where the nobleman has given everything, once he has presented his person, the bourgeois gives nothing, nor need he give anything through the medium of his person. The former can and must appear; the latter need only be, and his wishing to appear is ridiculous and absurd. The nobleman is a public personage . . . he is public by virtue of the representation that he embodies, and it is within that sphere that he takes on a personal aura. (Habermas 1989)

From around 1840 dress started to become standardised. The political reign of the bourgeoisie was beginning. The code of social appearances changed and neutrality was sought after. It was a similar imposture to the one by which the bourgeoisie sought to make its cultural order a universal order. The new code was based on a system of signs that drew on a boundless skill with detail. What a delight it is in this connection to read the pages of Balzac's *Autres études des femmes* in which the author describes with quite extraordinary meticulousness how it was still possible, between 1839 and 1842, to tell a female aristocrat and a woman of the bourgeoisie apart, the key being to pay attention 'to the little details'.

11 Miniaturisation

If you could not read a tie knot or the way a scarf was knotted around a bun, you could never tell with whom you were dealing (Sennet 1979).

People in the nineteenth century lived in a world where the rules governing dress were accessible only to the initiated. And the signs the initiated were able to decipher had arisen out of a process of miniaturisation ... If you did not know the rules governing that appearance, if you could not read a tie knot or the way a scarf was knotted around a bun, you could never tell with whom you were dealing. (Sennet 1979)

Between the private sphere and the public sphere the bourgeoisie erected a system of practices in which learning to recognise these distinguishing signs constituted an essential element. This bourgeois 'culture' was acquired and handed down, as we shall see, in the bosom of the family and in its educational appendages.

Subjected to ridicule and too aware of their diversity, today's bourgeois are unwilling to accept this generic name. However, as soon as they had set out the differences between the Xs and the Ys (thus, they felt, demonstrating the meaninglessness of the term), my informants did in fact, in the interplay of conversation and its concomitant exchange of viewpoints, well and truly acknowledge the existence of a bourgeois culture.

Despite the differences, we are bourgeois and recognised as such in terms of a code and in terms of a particular kind of upbringing that enables one not to run away despite misfortunes. (Mr Georges H. senior)

There was an element of coaxing, no doubt, but the same utterance came in different words from other 'bourgeois' mouths. The indigenous definition of the bourgeoisie stresses what is actually referred to as 'a culture'.

One is not bourgeois by virtue of one's job. I have a colleague who does the same job as I do. He is from a working-class background. His way of spending his money and his way of life bear no resemblance to mine. I believe the number one characteristic of the bourgeois milieu is possessing a shared moral conception, because economic import-ance is only secondary. That's how it is in my family. If there's a junior member who doesn't make it, say, one doesn't let them down. (Mr Pierre I. junior)

I am aware of belonging to a noteworthy and particularly gifted family. Turning out civilised individuals takes a certain education and many generations. (Mrs Laure C. senior)

One passes the test at table. One passes the test on the telephone. A bourgeois, what does that depend on, it doesn't depend on anything, it's a way of being, physically and mentally. (Mrs Pierre I. senior)

They're very subtle nuances: there may be a certain way of behaving socially in terms of 'that is just not done'. But it's not always the same in all milieux. There are words one does not say, grammatical mistakes one does not make. Upstarts [la bourgeoisie de promotion] are very careful not to say 'shit' because they think that is the done thing. But the nuances are subtler than that. (Mr Georges H. senior)

Education: there are particular values, moral and civil. In our families people developed the quality of leadership. There are the table manners of course, but to be civilised you need a long tradition handed down from generation to generation: a feeling for the refinement of culture and courtesy. (Mrs Laure C. senior)

It is not going too far out on a limb to say that the thing that has made it possible to focus on bourgeois culture today is the recent development of this social group. Let us conclude this introductory chapter with the example of the textile bourgeoisie of northern France. This is a bourgeoisie recognised by historians and by fellow bourgeois as specific and as representative of a pure and solid tradition. Cornuel and Duriez have studied the history of this northern French bourgeoisie. They note in their article that up until the beginning of the twentieth century it cannot be ranked as a caste. Its diversity was too great, its origins too heterogeneous. As the authors point out, however, after 1950 this bourgeoisie exhibited a clear tendency to close up. It began to deploy marriage strategies and to give itself an effective tool, namely the *Book of the Families of the Region of Northern France*,[6] which was to draw up bourgeois genealogies. The book served to itemise and define 'by name' the members that made up this textile bourgeoisie of northern France. It became a local society directory in the service of a sought-after endogamy. Today, the authors of this article conclude, the heirs of these industrial dynasties 'try that much harder to assert their joint membership of the bourgeoisie for the fact that their economic positions justify it less' (Cornuel and Duriez 1984).

Rid of the shadow that the aristocracy once cast over it and relieved of the

[6] *Le Livre des familles de la région du nord de la France*, published annually since 1912.

weight of a conception subordinating culture to praxis (a process that was facilitated by the loss of certain economic powers), the bourgeoisie is at last able to take stock of its cultural identity. It then becomes possible to listen to, watch and study the very people who for a great many complex reasons (glimpsed briefly during this chapter) have simultaneously hidden, denied their own existence and imposed themselves over the course of eight centuries of history.

# 3

## THE MAKING OF LAURE

### Laure

I first met Laure in June 1986. I knew from her answers to the questionnaire that she was married, was 32 years old, had two children and worked for the computer company run by her husband. A quick glance at the *Bottin mondain*[1] filled in her family background. She lives in the western suburbs.

I became very familiar, during the course of this study, with Paris's Saint-Lazare station, the terminus for trains to Saint-Cloud, Chaville, Vaucresson, Louveciennes, and Versailles – the affluent as well as verdant western suburbs of Paris. Most of these women had spent their childhoods in the eighth, sixteenth or seventeenth districts or in Neuilly. Now that they have moved outside the capital, they still (without realising it) occupy the same geographical area. Not long after marriage, very often on the birth of the second child, they left Paris to become the owners of enough space to accommodate their way of life (with a third child planned, a minimum of five or six rooms).

Laure lives in a large house surrounded by an enormous garden that lies behind a metal gate. Family backing (though the term seems inappropriate here; it is more like an advance against inheritance) made possible the acquisition of this residence, which the owner reckons at 'around 200 million old francs'.[2]

My first sight of Laure was of her standing on the threshold of her home, dressed in jeans. The broad collar of a pale pink blouse fell decoratively over a grey jumper of fine wool; on her feet, a pair of court shoes. Her straight, mid-length auburn hair had been hastily tied at the neck with a black velvet bow, exposing a sun-tanned face with little make-up. The third finger of her left hand bore an emerald set in diamonds. Laure was in casual dress; she was in fact supervising the laying of a carpet in the large living-room. Note,

---

[1] Published annually since 1903, this social directory currently lists some 43,000 families belonging to the aristocracy and the *haute bourgeoisie*. On the *Bottin mondain* and the *Livre des familles de la région du nord de la France*, see B. Le Wita (ed.), 'Cultures bourgeoises' issue of *Ethnologie française*, vol. 20, Paris (A. Colin), 1990. [B. L. W.]

[2] Approximately £200,000; the 'new franc' (= 100 'old francs') was introduced in 1960, but has yet to gain undisputed acceptance in the parlance of the old and the 'upper crust' [Tr.].

12 The making of Laure

'To grow up, the child must renounce what it is now for the as yet hazy outline of what it will become; but no one consents willingly to being dislodged from his positions and being guided by someone else. There is always some green elysium to be abandoned, some childhood realm to be left behind' (Léna 1981).

incidentally, one of the golden rules of bourgeois dress: even in its casual mode it enables the wearer to go out or to receive people without having to change. At half-past four Laure would slip into a navy-blue jacket to go and fetch her children from school.

That initial vision constituted a kind of ideal type. Indeed, Laure's appearance that day combined all the distinguishing marks to be spotted individually on most young women of her generation, give or take the odd variant (the jeans may be replaced by a straight skirt or kilt, for example, or the jumper by a cardigan).

The ring was the first element to catch my eye. I subsequently saw almost the same ring over and over again, adorning dozens of different hands. Sometimes it was a sapphire, sometimes an emerald; always it was surrounded by diamonds and set in white gold or platinum. Often the stone was a gift from a member of the family and the setting the choice of a fiancé. But beyond the resultant variations of detail, what strikes the observer is the uniformity of this 'little thing' worn in all circumstances.

Stamping the whole person in much the same way as the silver service on top of a cabinet or chest of drawers, this piece of jewellery is an obvious signal of membership of the bourgeois milieu. However, as my informants pointed out, 'the things that make a bourgeois are very under-stated nuances'. Take Laure's black velvet bow, for instance. This discreet sign of stylishness is acceptable because used in conjunction with hair that is left natural (not waved, for example, or worn in too original a cut). The almost imperceptible make-up reinforces the general impression of moderation or neutrality exuded by these young women.

There are jeans and jeans, one young informant told me.Indeed, bourgeois jeans (Laure's were a perfect example) are worn almost permanently with other garments that serve to obliterate the former's excessively adolescent, casual, fashionable character. Neutralising elements are shoes (delicate, low-heeled court shoes of dark leather) and a jumper of fine (cashmere) or medium (Shetland) wool obscuring the waist (i.e. hiding the label on the trousers), worn over an invariably pastel-coloured blouse of which only the collar is left showing. Like skirts ('neither mini nor maxi'), jeans must be in keeping with the physique of the wearer. Neither too tight, nor too baggy, nor too long, nor too short, 'bourgeois jeans' are also recognisable by the fact that they allow a glimpse of socks and ankles, emphasising the neutralising elements represented by moccasins or courts.

## Distinguishing marks

Neutralising means achieving the state of being neither one thing nor the other. Between the two negatives there unfolds an ample space that can be labelled *mediocritas*. 'Neither effeminate or soft, nor rough or rustic, neither

13 The ring

The ring was the first element to catch my eye. I subsequently saw almost the same ring over and over again, adorning dozens of different hands.

too slow nor too fast: that, said Cicero, is how the citizen's movements should be. *Mediocritas optima est'* (Schmitt 1978).

Like the opposite poles that, by attracting the balance, help it to find its equilibrium, elegance in the matter of civilities finds expression through the play of the double negative. One of the oldest traditions in the literature of good manners seeks to define this *mediocritas* that every civilised being should achieve. Desiderius Erasmus and Jean-Baptiste de La Salle, to mention only the best-known authors of handbooks of civility, address themselves to all children without distinction of rank. They put forward a presentation of self and a kind of self-control that will provide opportunities for social exchange. A person should in fact succeed in erasing his idiosyncracies in order that any physical expression should be recognisable by the greatest number. To that end, a system of attitudes was worked out on the basis of the notion of the 'happy medium'. As a result, 'the private sphere was taken into account only in order to be manipulated and made to conform to a model which is that of the happy medium, the rejection of every form of excess' (Revel 1986). The project was coloured by an almost anthropological ambition, proposing as it did to base the social tie on the acquisition by learning of a code of behaviour common to all. And the aristocracy was quite right to see the need to learn as evidence of non-education. The well-bred man does not learn good manners; he receives them as a gift or through grace. Down the centuries, the learning of manners became the favourite butt of anti-bourgeois satire.

Today, however, the bourgeois readily present their education as 'second nature'. If the project of a code of behaviour common to the whole social body came to nothing, the illusion on which it was based lived on. The proof lay in the way in which the bourgeois regarded their rules of correct behaviour as representing a certain minimum state to which every civilised being must attain. Idiosyncracies remained, however, making *mediocritas* the special property of the bourgeoisie.

The classic elements of the bourgeois outfit are a tweed or flannel suit, straight or pleated skirt, kilt, blouse, cardigan, cashmere or Shetland wool jumper, loden coat or jacket, moccasins or court shoes, scarf and a small shoulder bag. They do not change with fashion. One knows where to buy them. They can thus be made to circulate among people, even between generations. Order reigns in the private relationship between a woman and her body. Various scarves and accessories embellish and personalise these outfits. But never do bourgeois clothes serve to express idiosyncratic behaviour. On the contrary, they conform to what a women should present of herself. In this way they create an element of distinction, understood in the sense of separation (separating, for example, bourgeois jeans from other jeans).

This sartorial imperative, inculcated from birth, suggests that it does not form the object of any learning process. People will use tradition to account

14 Behind the Silver Cross pram

One's dress is in keeping with the proper presentation of oneself. It does not serve to express idiosyncratic behaviour.

for behaviours that really do 'go without saying'. 'Culture is in contrast to nature yet readily thinks of itself as natural' (Pouillon 1975).

With their mastery of the art of detail that will distinguish them and at the same time hallow them in an almost ritual manner, bourgeois women quietly 'stand out' in the urban throng. The way they dress testifies to the fact that they belong to the milieu. More precisely, it is intuitively identified as such by peers. Indeed, it may be that the sought-after distinction does not so much operate in relation to the Other; above all it enables the *bourgeoise* to recognise and be recognised by her own people. What we have here is a set of subtle but effective tokens at a time in history when dress no longer officially indicates social standing. So it is that, out here in the suburbs, away from their childhood homes in Paris, these young women spot one another at the school gate or in the market and swiftly reconstitute their micro-milieu. Bridge-playing, exhibition-going, and exchanging services connected with the children subsequently cement contacts that were initially experienced as chance encounters, enabling those involved to believe that they do indeed 'frequent all milieux'.

Similarly, having this 'innate' understanding of the code of appearances, young people at university or at the *grandes écoles* naturally 'make the right friends'. Mr Georges H. junior said he had managed to escape 'marriage by ball' but not this law of recognition/attraction.

It sounds silly, but when I first set eyes on my wife at college I recognised her. At the time, in 1967, she was the classic bourgeois young lady: hair in buns at the back of the neck, silk blouse, concealed pearl necklace, blue cardigan buttoned up, kilt, stockings, court shoes.

Simply listing (and the list would inevitably be incomplete) the elements that go to make up bourgeois dress does not explain what it is that makes a particular young woman, seen in the street, identifiable as bourgeois. This was just where the example of Laure seemed apposite in that she was wearing jeans that day, in other words a garment common to a fairly broad spectrum of society. So one's eye was able to practise picking out what it was that distinguished Laure from other young women.

The example of Florence would have been equally apposite, although in her case it was the face and hair one needed to focus on. Florence has an elongated face marked by a clearly outlined mouth revealing perfect teeth. Her straight hair is square-cut with a parting at the side. Sometimes worn dyed (dark blond, streaked or auburn), it vigorously echoes the movements of her head and body. Florence was wearing a loose-fitting beige raincoat (open) with padded shoulders, a Hermès scarf around her neck, costume jewellery, a shoulder bag slung across her body, black or navy stockings, and court shoes. You might come across Florence dressed like that in the rue de Rennes, for example, in Paris's sixth district, late one weekday morning.

In this case distinction (the act of separating or the condition of that which is separate) is the result of a subtle balance between what a women allows to be glimpsed of herself and what she keeps concealed. Any attempt to put into words this nature shaped by culture (in the interests of 'looking natural') will find it very hard to get away from the rhetorical figures of the double negative and the association of opposites: light make-up allowing the texture of the skin and the colour of the complexion to show through, natural hair that is nevertheless cut and styled, firm yet relaxed tone of voice, clear but restrained gestures. Never at the cutting edge of fashion, these women look timeless without ever being out of period, as it were. Like the pastel colours they favour, their general appearance inspires what might be called a feeling of permanence.

However, this state of *mediocritas*, divine though it may appear, is learned and handed down. It calls for an education based on self-control and

15 Appearing natural

Distinction stems from a subtle balance between what one reveals and what one conceals of oneself.

presupposes almost a ritualisation of daily life. Things do indeed need to be organised, people need to be organised in order to become, to impose, and to institute the subject in her status as 'bourgeois'. This mastery is acquired by way of control of the relations between individual and collective interests.

Bourgeois education, like any other kind of apprenticeship, is based on a constant state of tension and restraint meticulously offset against areas of freedom. The way in which today's bourgeoisie tends to crystallise its physical and moral mode of being seems to be in response to a fragility born of its historical mobility and variability. It could, for example, be said that the bourgeoisie has never been more bourgeois than today. By virtue of a kind of privilege of seniority it is able, now, to have us overlook the fact that the origins of its distinction (as a privileged social group) lie in function and wealth, recreating the old conception of privilege, that of being simply an 'entitlement'. The bourgeoisie today claims moral qualities attaching to the individual. 'Having three generations of wing collars behind one', as Mr Georges H. junior put it, is enough for the collective memory to turn into a quality what is actually, in origin, a mere acquisition. However, lest anyone should think the bourgeois can do what he likes, note how Elias reflects simply that 'the bourgeois is someone under constant self-constraint' (Elias 1974).

Certainly the domestic intimacy, the presence of other generations, the ease of access to social rules that are always being made explicit, and the breadth of the kinship networks and material affluence enjoyed by these families produce a feeling of security that enables a person not to fall victim to the vagaries of individual fate. But these essential guarantees are not the whole story. A person must also master and internalise certain restrictive norms. The bourgeois believe that their culture (or what they are) should be shared by all. They are naïvely unaware of what makes them special. They see their table manners, for example, simply in terms of a 'minimum level' of politeness. One learns not to do certain things (eat with one's mouth open, for instance) and to do others (raise the arm to lift a glass to one's lips) purely out of respect for oneself and others. It is 'simple kindness', they will say.

When the Sainte Marie de Passy College moved to Rueil, one could spot the new recruits by the way they dressed and by their table manners: they ate just anyhow.

Lorraine was evidently sensitive to these distinguishing marks. Yet when she brought home a boyfriend of unknown provenance and her mother announced several days later that they could not have him again since he behaved badly at table, Lorraine thought this 'intolerant'. It was in contradiction, she felt, to her parents' Christian principles of generosity. Lorraine was bearing witness to the difficult balance to be struck between individual interests (that of a friend who was 'not one of us') and collective interests (harmony within the family and social group). Without any malice it could be added that Lorraine's latest boyfriend, whom she had come across by chance in Holland, passed the 'table test' brilliantly. Lacking any fixed occupation, he was nevertheless the son of a naval officer.

They may seem merely anecdotal, but Lorraine's remarks enable us to put our finger on vital elements of the transmission of values within the bourgeoisie. Even here, nothing runs smoothly. For instance, it may go without saying for parents to send their daughters to the Sainte Marie colleges, but it does not go without saying that the daughters will stay there without at least once expressing a desire to 'get out' and 'see somewhere else'. Remember the fascination that R. Garric held for Simone de Beauvoir and many other young women of her generation (see above, p. 46).

Most of the time, internalisation of the constraints passes through this kind of rejection stage. There is no reproduction without hesitations and hitches. Marie-Cécile, a 38-year-old television producer, set out determinedly, between the ages of 20 and 30, to break out of her family and social environment. Among other affairs, she lived with a working-class man and bore him a daughter; she subsequently left him and at the time of the interview was living with 'a fringe artist'. Her way of life, which had also involved a break with religion, was severely condemned by the family at large. She was even banned from the family seat, though she was never, she said, left without material support. 'One doesn't let them down.' At the end of the interview she said in some vexation:

Currently, in the whirlpool world of television, living with a man of different social origins, I have the impression of living amid such upheaval that I have very few landmarks. And I'm ultimately very grateful to my background and to Sainte Marie for having provided me with a solid foundation. However, the reason why I live with people who are self-educated whereas I am all determinisms is that I never had the opportunity to go and look anywhere else. Between twenty and now I've become hyper-aware of the fact that I cannot do without my milieu; I'm a bourgeois and glad to be one.

## Bourgeois culture

Three factors seem capable of accounting for this bourgeois culture: the art of detail, self-control or a controlled internalisation, and the ritualisation of everyday existence providing a passage from the private sphere to the public sphere.

### The art of detail

The attention given to detail may be seen as the end result of a lengthy process setting the bourgeoisie against the habits of the Ancien Régime. We have mentioned several times how the aristocrat shows what he is, and how that is sufficient. In this code of appearances 'trifles' (Elias uses the word *bagatelles*) have precise meanings. The aristocrat (in the 'global' represen-tation of his public persona) quite clearly attaches enormous importance to details. However, they form part of a complex of signs leading to instanta-neous recognition of a person's quality. The details of the bourgeois person's mode of being are for their part aimed at discretion and neutrality – at 'not showing off'.

It is tempting to draw a parallel between the development of the methods according to which the power to punish was exercised and the emergence of the bourgeois persona. Punishment under monarchical law gave rise to 'a ceremony, a spectacle that could be sight-read, as it were' (Foucault 1975). The same author states that at the end of the eighteenth century a 'coercive, corporal, solitary, secret model was to replace the representative, theatrical, signifying, public model'. At the centre of his proof is the detail, the 'little thing'.

Discipline, he goes on, is 'a political anatomy of detail'. Interest in these little things did not originate in the eighteenth century. Rather a whole philosophical tradition of the infinitely small runs throughout history.

In any case, detail had for a long time been a category of theology and asceticism. Every detail is important, since in the eyes of God there is no vastness greater than a detail, nor is anything so small as not to have been willed by an individual wish of his. (*ibid.*)

The *âge classique* [seventeenth and early eighteenth centuries] was to extend this 'microphysics' of power, this fixation on detail, to the whole body of society. The school was to become one of the main places where this 'hymn to little things' resounded. When later in this chapter we come to look at the Sainte Marie colleges, we shall see how, despite wearing a uniform, girls learn to read the minutest signs in order to distinguish social micro-groups in a quite densely homogeneous world.

### Self-control

This attention to the details and nuances that make up the whole person is inseparable from the idea of self-control. Bourgeois asceticism is a mode of conduct aimed at overcoming the *status naturae*, removing man from the power of instinct, and freeing him from his dependence upon the world and nature. What Max Weber recognised as specific to Lutheranism is not in fact far from the kind of Catholic bourgeois asceticism that was inspired by Jesuit thought.

The most urgent task: control of self with a view to destroying the ingenuity of the spontaneous power of instinct; the most powerful means: putting some order into individual behaviour. (Weber 1964)

Hahn draws a comparison in his work on the sociology of confession between the growth in the internal and external control of the self described by Elias as part of the process of civilisation and the religious roots that also lie at the origin of this notion of self-control. If in the context of politics and court life the process of self-control led people to conceal what they were and what they did, while in the religious context the same process led to a disciplining of the emotions and to self-knowledge, 'the object was the same, namely to discipline and control the instincts' (Hahn 1986).

This control of the internal mechanisms governing a person's private and public conduct is something that is acquired. In the privacy of his family and the social relations that go with that world the bourgeois moves through life, finding on his way certain landmarks or reference points that then become his *habitus*. Everyday life is made up of a succession of acts, gestures and habits sufficiently codified to be classed as rituals.

## Ritualised everyday practices

The bourgeoisie's 'done thing', like tradition's 'such and such has always been done', indicates the establishment of a cultural space around practices that need to be kept under constant supervision. It would perhaps be superfluous to dwell at length on the meaning to be given to the word 'rite'. Two quotations will define the way in which it is used here. Both stress the social function of the rite.

In a religious world as in civil societies, they [rites] serve to reiterate and strengthen ties, occasionally giving expression to conflicts in order to transcend them (which raises the problem of successes and levels of integration), and also to renew and refresh beliefs, to propagate the ideas of a culture and give them form (which refers to a cognitive dimension), to define roles, and to try to structure in terms of behaviour the way in which a society or social group sees itself. (Rivière 1983)

[The rite serves] to separate those who have undergone it not from those who have not undergone it but rather from those who do not undergo it in any way and thus to institute lasting differences between those the rite concerns and those it does not. (Bourdieu 1982)

From the learning of table manners, through which the child acquires control over its gestures, its appetite (never help yourself to more food unless invited to do so by the mistress of the house) and its words (everyone must be able to have his or her say) to, for example, the coming-out ball, we are undoubtedly looking at a series of ritual practices. Table manners (everyday practices) and balls (occasional practices) serve to strengthen ties, to perpetuate the group's ideas and modes of conduct, to distribute roles and places, and to confirm individual status. This is why concentrating on table manners is in fact quite a useful exercise. Mealtimes are consciously experienced as a special moment of socialisation around which the whole complex of the distinguishing marks of the bourgeois family group becomes focused and is handed down. This explains why little Edouard's mother can no longer have the caretaker's son at her 'canteen lunches': 'I feel too sorry for him, he behaves like a pig.' Most of the time there is no problem because the children always meet the same kind of children and learn without realising they are learning (Le Wita and Sjögren 1987(a)). In the bourgeoisie, as Sjögren points out, the ritual of the meal has undergone a profound transformation between the nineteenth century and the present. Last century's *comme il faut* ['the right way'] is giving way to today's *comme il nous convient* ['the way that suits us'].

The action of the meal remains none the less essential in the cultural training of the group by contributing to the learning of roles, to family solidarity, and to social distribution. (Sjögren 1986)

Invited to 'take pot luck' at everyday lunches and dinners, I was able to observe these little nothings, these famous details that testify to bourgeois culture. Eaten in the kitchen with the couple and their children all present, the meal proceeds swiftly and simply. However, the *petits suisses* are eaten with silver teaspoons, each egg cup has a history, the goblet Mathilde is drinking from was a present from her grandmother, the bread is broken and placed in a basket, the younger child is told not to put its elbows on the table, not to get down yet, not to rush, and not to keep others waiting. The whole thing takes place in a brisk yet orderly manner. The basic principles are distilled consistently and insistently but without anyone getting cross.

An invitation to a family meal with not just the parents but also cousins and the rest of the clan present strikes the observer as special proof of acceptance. Generally speaking, no stranger is permitted to share this type of meal without some thought (one has no wish to expose the group to the risk of being embarrassed by unusual, different forms of behaviour). So when you are invited you know you have been credited with being able to conform to the rules of the group. This is an initiation ordeal (you are penetrating the family's privacy). And you learn in this way that while the rules and customs are the common property of all 'well-bred' people, they also form the object of local adaptations, with each family seeking to develop its special characteristics. The observer needs to be able to spot these swiftly (you have to know, for example, that great-grandfather used to cut his salad with a knife). In fact these special characteristics are no more than minor infringements of the rules. They are a way of showing that one is not afraid to take liberties on the fringes of the code. A ritual exists only if the members of the group are in a position to designate its limits. The group demonstrates an attachment to such trifles, which represent as it were the family's idiosyncracies. In a world in which self-representation gives rise to codified and identifiable scenarios, these signs allow the group a feeling of originality and enable it to be named and recognised for its own sake.

16 Mrs O. senior's drawing-room

In this cultural space, relationships with others are forged and unfold. A person must know how to move in a closed world.

What is originality? To see something that does not yet have a name, that cannot yet exist although there for everyone to see. The way men usually are, it is only the name of the thing that begins to make it visible to them. (Nietzsche, *Joyful Wisdom*)

Such details nourish the system of in-jokes underlying the expression *pièces rapportées* [see p. 47]: the daughter-in-law will formally record, for example, that the Xs (surname of the in-law family) eat their stewed fruit with a fork. Generally speaking, these little nothings are part of the diversity of the bourgeois milieu. In the cultural space thus created, relationships with others are forged and unfold. A person must know how to move in a closed world. Rules of dress and politeness and table manners common to this milieu are thus embellished with imaginative touches to provide a backcloth that is always unique. And we shall see how family memory feeds on these peculiarities, perpetuating them and erecting them into veritable symbols.

However, modes of behaviour certainly comply with a very strict code. They form a system and give rise to such precise scenarios that we may attempt to describe them through the medium of two customs: the drawing-room and how to negotiate it, and the summons to sit down to eat [*passer à table*]. These two moments of bourgeois family life also serve as initiation ordeals in that the outsider, not knowing the rules, is immediately and implicitly spotted as such.

17 Mrs O. junior's drawing-room

The youngster running in from the garden will be restrained by a look and a few kind words.

To negotiate a drawing-room a child, say, needs to know how to move with neither hesitation nor undue haste but easily and quietly through a space that is organised for the adult world. This means, for example, walking behind the armchairs grouped around the coffee tables, not taking just any seat but knowing instinctively which of them one may occupy (above all, not taking the most comfortable), and moderating one's utterance and controlling one's movements to show respect for the world of the 'grown-ups' who have gathered there to talk or to relax. The youngster running in from the garden at full tilt or tumbling down from his room will be restrained by a look and a few kind words. The very arrangement of the furniture (coffee table, armchairs and settee, objects, carpet) traces possible paths and dictates appropriate attitudes. Direct access to the grown-ups sitting there is made difficult; very often the child can only lean on the back of a chair or present a side view. He will be taken by the forearm and invited to stand in front of the person he wishes to see. In this way he learns to master the transition from outside to inside, to pass gradually from agitation to calm, from chatter to controlled speech.

Another ordeal is the moment of sitting down to eat. The summons to do so gives rise to a curious scene. Having entered the dining-room, the group will come to a halt a little way from the table. There can be no question of people just sitting anywhere and taking their places before the hostess arrives. She,

18 The family meal
One prolonged rule of politeness in which each party apologises for holding everyone else up.

however, is coming and going between dining-room and kitchen, supervising the final arrangements for the meal. So between the moment when people leave the drawing-room and the time when they are finally seated at the table there is an ill-defined, difficult period with the potential for generating disorder. The individual suddenly finds himself plunged into relative solitude, isolated in his individuality. Psychological skills and levels of integration in the group will govern each person's attitudes. Some will drift together by affinity and chat freely, giving the impression of 'having something to say to one another'; others will appear more timid, readily associating with the person who will be sitting next to them during the meal. Every member of the group shares in the emptiness of the moment. The scene might be compared to one prolonged rule of politeness in which each party apologises for holding everyone else up. Circling the table discreetly, everybody waits without attempting to do anything. Then the hostess makes her 'final' entrance, indicating that the meal can commence. The allocation of places, quietly indicated by the hostess, is organised along conventional lines, depending on the number of family members foregathered and the presence or not of outsiders. This ceremony only takes place, of course, on the occasion of large family reunions; in the privacy of the home each person knows his or her place.

Without such ritualisations, neither good manners nor self-control can truly be acquired. Alongside these customs governing everyday life, a series of balls [called *rallyes* in French] constitute an exceptional kind of ritual strictly controlling successive stages of childhood and adolescence.

Take the adolescence of Laure C. junior, now 32. At the age of 12 she began with what is called the 'Jam Ball' [*Rallye confiture*]. 'The first year', she told me, 'there were no boys. One outing a month was organised on Sunday afternoon (excursions in Paris, museums).' The next year brought the 'Bridge Ball' [*Rallye bridge*], when boys were first involved. A year was spent learning to play bridge. 'There was also a tea party ending at seven o'clock, that was once a month.' Next Laure C. attended dancing lessons 'at Baraduc's in the rue de Ponthieu' (virtually all the young ladies I met had attended this establishment, listed in the *Bottin mondain* [see footnote 1, p. 62] as offering 'society dancing lessons'). In Laure C.'s words:

It's brilliant, there are two large rooms with polished floors and mirrors. On one side: thirty girls in their Sunday best, facing thirty boys in suits and patent-leather shoes. In the middle a dancing master teaching us rock and the waltz.

As the wife of Georges H. junior commented: 'At Baraduc's one learned to dance like going to school. Imagine two Gaffios[3] between you and your partner.'

After Baraduc's, Laure C. junior graduated to more serious pursuits, namely parties [*boums*].

It was always the girls who gave them. One got a card: X will be at home from 6 to 11 p.m. The mothers were in a drawing-room. Later there was the eight-to-midnight with sound system and long dresses. And finally the super-dos, the balls.

These are held in one's town house or on hired premises (the 'pavillon d'Armenonville', for example, or the 'Cercle de l'Union interallié', or 'le Pré Catelan', or 'le Tir aux pigeons'). They are real celebrations.

At 6 in the morning breakfast is served. A good ball (so far as the mothers are concerned) is the one where there are the most names with handles and the most dough. One's supposed to meet people. Balls serve to create a suitable environment. On the door one is asked for one's invitation and identity card. The fellows are prats, spoilt, over-protected, pretentious, totally inexperienced. I did eventually make some friends, four or five people I still see. (Laure C. junior)

Georges H. junior, who is ten years older than Laure C. junior, gave this account:

In Paris there are certain leading families (aristocracy plus dough) who have managed to freshen themselves up with the top bourgeoisie. One must entertain. One must go to the Pré Catelan, to the pavillon d'Armenonville. But the absolute must is entertaining at home. I remember one marvellous ball in a mansion near the Etoile. So there's a certain overlap between the historic bourgeoisie and the moneyed aristocracy. As a

---

3   I.e. fat dictionaries, specifically Professor F. Gaffio's Latin–French dictionary for schools, which is 7 cm thick (making the required distance between dancing partners 14 cm!).

result there are a number of good ladies who conspire together to marry off their little girls, heads of families, silly rich bitches. If a girl has passed 21 and hasn't nailed a fellow yet, she's got problems. In Paris there are eighty families one can associate with. The age of vulgarity has gradually crept in with the business of the identity card at the door.

Mrs Georges H. junior had this to say:

I gave a ball with my girlfriend L. I remember Mummy saying she was prepared [in 1967] to spend 500,000 francs for the *petits fours*. If success can be measured in terms of money spent, mine was a middling ball, in terms of names with handles, too. But a ball is basically no more exotic than a local hop.

Emilie E., now 20, gave and attended numerous balls between the ages of 15 and 19. They were 'among the poshest in Paris'. Quite properly, she first passed through Baraduc's.

Some balls are posher than others, the poshest being also the most exclusive. The parents giving the ball are there, and you're asked for your invitation and identity card. A barker announces you. You bow to the parents and say hello to the girl who is entertaining that evening. Afterwards you look for friends whom you know. You drink, you dance. Balls last from 8 in the evening to 6 in the morning. The fellows are awful, morons and pimply youths with triple-barrelled names. At the Xs' ball the whole Parisian upper crust was there (the d'Estaing and Murat families, the Prince of Yugoslavia, the Perreires, Colgate toothpaste, the lot). One knows the names, the parents are more or less acquainted with one another. One always knows who's who. I went to balls every Saturday for two years. They're pretty fantastic: the décor, the drink, the music. There were some lavish dos in some of the châteaux around Paris, with fabulous buffets.

These balls bring boys and girls face to face who may one day marry. Flirtation is all; sexual relations are banned.

There are taboos. A girl must not tease or be provocative. If a girl has sexual relations with boys, people say: 'The whole of Paris has been over her bar the Underground,' (Emilie E.)

Georges H. junior dismissed the whole ball scene with such expressions as 'the reign of the half-virgins' [except that English uses the French insult *demi-vierges*] and 'synchronised tummy-rubbing', while his wife said they were 'merely an attempt on the part of the bourgeois families to keep dancing within bounds'.

In fact they represent an initiatory stage during which the young man or woman enters his or her milieu. Mother-controlled relations constitute the social capital of the future bourgeois man or woman. Sexuality 'in abeyance' is sexuality under control. 'Between having a party and actually doing it, there is a real barrier. One pretends. One goes through the motions' (Mr Georges H. junior). Usually it is not at the end of this stage that people get married. The future husband and wife will meet 'by chance' somewhere else but will in fact previously have attended the same functions.

*Madame...*                    *Monsieur...*                    *Madame...*

*recevront pour leurs filles*

*Diane*                          *Coralie*                          *Delphine*

*le samedi 24 mai 1986 à 21 heures*
*dans les Salons de l'Académie Diplomatique Internationale*
*4 bis, avenue Hoche, Paris VIII^e*

*Tenue de Soirée - Invitation et carte d'identité demandées à l'entrée*

19 The ball (photo published in Paris-Presse 1964)
'Some balls are posher than others, the poshest being also the most exclusive' (Miss Emilie E.).

Not all bourgeois families participate in 'the ball system'. There is of course a whole set of social distinctions between those who entertain, those who are invited but never entertain, and those who will never be invited. But among families of comparable social standing, some reject these extravagant rituals in the name of an ethic of moderation. In this case other forms of controlled activity are offered to the younger generation. Take the example of Pierre I. junior, who told me:

The way my wife and I met forms part of the education of the bourgeoisie. I was 17, she was 13 years old. There was a course of dancing lessons, a group of thirty people. A teacher came to our house to teach us to dance the waltz, rock, and the tango. The schools were not mixed, one knew one's female cousins but had no girls who were friends. So the mother of a girl and the mother of a boy would organise this dancing course. There were sixy of us and we used to dance in four rooms. The furniture was moved out. Then we met again subsequently on the basis of being kindred spirits. We formed a group of twelve friends, went skiing and so on.

Table manners and balls do not exhaust these ritual practices. Many others survive. Politeness, the cornerstone of bourgeois behaviour, is one of them – and not the least important, either. How one greets people, how one introduces oneself, how one says thank you, and how one expresses feelings form a cultural concentrate that balances proximity against the distance that must be maintained in relation to other people.

To round off this presentation of bourgeois culture, let us look at fragments of a conversation in which the three ideas we have been considering (the art of detail, self-control and the ritualisation of everyday life) find themselves organised in a curious coherence.

Geneviève, a 38-year-old sociologist, had all her schooling at Sainte Marie de Neuilly. She went around with her classmates there but never regarded them as close friends:

It was later when I met them again [always this impression of a free choice, you notice], I realised that it was very important, our having attended the same school, received the same education. One shares winks, certain spontaneous reactions. One sees people in the same way, little things but they count for an awful lot. For instance, my boyfriend S. [Geneviève is living with a man, having previously been married and divorced] is an individualist. One of my girlfriends, also a Sainte Marie old girl, reacts to that individualism in the same way I do. I wasn't brought up to do as I please. I decide to do what pleases me, but I don't let myself go. For example, we're invited to the Xs', it's all planned. In the mean time someone offers us something else that's more fun. S. will go for the thing that's more fun. But if I commit myself to something I make sure it happens. It's a chicken-and-egg situation, I know. I always feel responsible. It's a conception one has of oneself within society.

Elsewhere in the same interview, Geneviève said:

We had a fine house with a garden in Neuilly, with one or two permanent staff. We lived well, but the main thing was not to spoil the children. Life spoiled us, though.

20  The three generations

'Mother entertains for her daughter with grandmother tenderly looking on. This was in 1964.
Mummy was giving a party for my seventeenth birthday. In 1989 I shall be giving a party for my
daughter's seventeenth birthday' (Mrs O. junior).

The family circle is concerned to integrate the child in the social ethic of the
group to which it belongs. The individual is initiated into what he or she is
and must become.

The institution of an identity, which may be a title of nobility or a stigma ('you're
nothing but a ...'), is the imposition of a name, that is to say a social essence.
Initiating, allotting an essence, a competence, involves imposing a right to be that is
also a responsibility. That means informing a person of what he is and telling him that
he must behave accordingly. (Bourdieu 1982)

## The education of girls at the Sainte Marie colleges

As in many other social groups, the bourgeois woman plays a crucial role in
the organisation of family life. She is in a position to pass on the basic features
of the group culture. Not the least of her functions will be to soothe the
tensions that arise out of the constraints necessary to reproducing the status.
It is the mother who will keep the child, sometimes against its will, in the
chosen educational structures, to which end she will make several visits to
shed tears in headteachers' offices. It is she, too, who will give it firm guidance
in the ways of good behaviour. She will also manage the child's leisure
activities, readily assuming the role of taxi driver to take this one to riding
lessons every Wednesday, say, or that one to a tea party. She will take great
care not to get 'out of touch', allowing her daughter a limited period of

rebellion against pleated skirts, for instance. Thus the musical or otherwise exquisitely cultured grandmother does not merely symbolise the maternal world in which the distinguishing marks are acquired almost by heredity; she is also, as regards the bourgeois persona, a vision of humanity throwing open the gates of the imagination. In short, such women create Baudelaire's 'green elysium of childhood loves'. And since they are considered essential to the good order of family society, how they are educated is decisive. The bourgeois milieu prefers education to be handed down rather than acquired (having generations of civilised men and women behind one constitutes a solid guarantee). The duties of these women are commensurate with the powers that the group confers on them. And to fit them for their function they are deliberately cast in a certain psychological and physical mould. (This is why, incidentally, the women we interviewed seemed more accessible to ethnographic study than the men.) Trying to understand the educational structures within which they grew up (hence this study of the Sainte Marie colleges) will help us to see how a person becomes Laure.

*Marthe and Marie-Christine*

Two interviews (out of a total of some fifty undertaken) provide an introduction to the world of the Sainte Marie colleges.

Marthe and Marie-Christine are both former pupils of Sainte Marie de Passy. Their accounts portray dissimilar experiences of life. Marthe, aged 34, comes across as a person who, during and after her Sainte Marie schooling, was forever 'poking her nose in elsewhere'. The 32-year-old Marie-Christine, on the other hand, exemplifies the considered career of a young woman 'perfectly in tune with the Sainte Marie spirit'. Respecting these differences brings out in a quite striking way the characteristic features of this educational system.

'You were there [at Sainte Marie] to do your duty' is how Marthe put it at the beginning of the interview. There could be no clearer expression of the early imposition of the idea of duty (although a certain amount of bedlam was also involved, as were forbidden games, whispers that went round the class, giggling during silent retreats, and so on; the interiorisation of standards was accomplished by way of a healthy management of seemingly contradictory attitudes).

Marthe's father is a company chairman and belongs to a family of doctors (great-grandfather and grandfather) and people of private means. He attended a Catholic boarding-school in Bayonne. Marthe's mother comes of a family of managers of large estates in Algeria and Tunisia. The move to the colonies took place after the family fortune had been squandered by her great-grandfather. She was educated by the Ursulines and belongs to a family with (according to Marthe) a very strong religious tradition.

My maternal grandmother was extremely religious. She belonged to a para-religious order that was devoted to God. I have an aunt who entered a convent of the order of Saint Clare at eighteen. My mother was rather reserved. For her the religious habitus [Marthe is a sociologist] is an act of loyalty to her mother. My father was more of a non-believer and did not come to mass every Sunday.

(This distinction between a very pious branch whose religious principles permeate everyday life and a so-called 'conventional Catholic' branch, is a very common one.)

Marthe had her primary schooling at La Tour, a private school in the rue de la Pompe, which was near her parents' home. 'They didn't for one moment ask whether I should go anywhere else,' she said. When Marthe was in the *septième* her mother decided that she should enter the *sixième* at Sainte Marie.[4] 'Saint Marie had the reputation of having the intellectual cream. The difference between La Tour and Sainte Marie was the latter's 98 per cent baccalauréat pass rate.' To send her there her mother had to make three visits to the principal's office, because it is not easy to get into a Sainte Marie college. Marthe passed her end-of-year exam and entered the sixth class at Sainte Marie de Passy in 1963.

There was a change of uniform, I went from grey to navy blue. I was enrolled in section A, Latin, Greek, German. My father had done the same. German because Europe was just beginning, and being a difficult language it had to be learned first; Greek was for the civilisation; for English I would simply go to England.

Marthe very soon found the social atmosphere oppressive. 'They talked about friends of friends of cousins.' The aristocracy and the upper bourgeoisie dominated, imposing criteria of distinction between girls. Like most of her friends, Marthe very quickly learned to spot the countless varieties of *bourgeoises*.

In the aristocracy, there is the hard-up kind and the kind that belongs to the jet set; in the bourgeoisie, there is the very traditional kind where the girls work hard and are ugly, they're the future sisters of Sainte Marie. In our set we tended to use them, we tormented them rather. Socially, they're more modest than the others. And there's also the very modern kind of bourgeoisie with foreign marriages, they're the trendies. In between there's a traditional bourgeoisie, closer to the penniless aristocracy basically.

Marthe sets herself apart, creating a new sub-category for the occasion: 'I was closer to the very modern kind of bourgeoisie with a bit less money but slightly more than the traditional kind.' Every single interview touched on such micro-divisions: one was always less than, more than, or about the same as some other kind of bourgeois. The 18-year-old Eléonore, talking about a

---

[4]  The *septième* is equivalent to what in England is now called Year 6 (10 year olds, more or less), the *sixième* to Year 7, and so on. *Première* is the old lower sixth, now Year 12, and *terminale* the last year of secondary schooling in which pupils sit their *baccalauréat*, the school-leaving examination providing access to higher education [Tr.].

21 Sainte Marie de Neuilly, 1957

Like most of her friends, Marthe very quickly learned to detect the countless varieties of bourgeoisie.

school photograph, listed no fewer than nine categories of bourgeois: not very bourgeois, discreet bourgeois, very bourgeois, very bourgeois-very BCBG,[5] hyper-trendy bourgeois, petit bourgeois, Sainte Marie vintage bourgeois, super-bourgeois, toff [*aristo*].

Like most of her friends, Marthe believes that the uniform did not cover up these differences. The girls had to wear a navy-blue skirt or slacks, a white blouse, and a navy-blue pinafore pulled on over the head. Make-up had to be discreet, and jewellery was forbidden. Marthe's verdict on this uniform is that 'it was a complete con'. Girls very quickly learned to spot the little details that give away degrees of wealth and of conformity to the rules of the milieu.

One knew whether clothes were new or not, whether a jumper was hand-knitted or not, whether Burlingtons [shoes] were genuine or imitation, whether a raincoat came

---

5 *Bon-chic-bon-genre* (pronounced 'bay-say-bay-zhay'). In England, 'Sloane ranger' is approximately equivalent. 'BCBG: In fact, and in terms of very complex standards, it refers to everything that distinguishes those who know from those who do not, the aristocracy and the ancient bourgeoisie from the rest, the new rich from the old rich (especially those who have now fallen on hard times, which is of only relative importance since they are "BCBG").' (From the Introduction to Thierry Hantoux, *Guide du BCBG*, Paris [Hermé]), 1985)

22  Sainte Marie de Neuilly, 1984

'School uniform is one big con' (Marthe).

from Old England, Burberrys, or Halphen. And then at mass pinafores were not worn, so you could see how girls were dressed.

Marthe says Sainte Marie left her untouched intellectually.

Culturally it's the pits. We had these thinking days. I remember one on Marx, for instance. It was peanuts. [...] The modern world meant Catholic youth groups and the missionary angle.

Marthe remembers only one thing: 'fooling around was just not on'.

The main thing at Sainte Marie, she says, was to 'have the spirit' [*avoir l'esprit*]; the expression was used all the time there.

At Sainte Marie a person might be thought fit to move up each year if she was well-behaved and if she showed evidence of group spirit, responsibility, values that were taken as much into account as your marks. In your report book you had: behaviour in the group, individual behaviour, work.

In 1968 Marthe underwent an adolescent crisis.

I was fed up. I had lost my faith. I was fed up with being two years ahead. The nuns wouldn't let me retake a year. I was interested in clothes, boys, records.

Like most of her friends, Marthe suffered from being imprisoned between her family and school.

One was in a hurry to leave. My mother cried, so I stayed for the sake of peace. But it was suffocating. One never left the sixteenth district. I went to a café in the place du Trocadéro mornings in the fifth form. At lunchtime, too. It was the big thrill in my life. I had a boyfriend who came to fetch me at the end of school. I was tremendously pleased with myself. My mother knew. It was a calculated move to get at the bigots, not so much the nuns. I had a pretty free relationship with my parents. Over the uniform business, mother was on my side. But at the academic level I was told I mustn't drop out. I was programmed to work, to go on to college or university.

The break came:

After doing my *hypo-cagne*[6] at Henri IV I left to go to university. Lycée was still too much for me. At the philosophy faculty at Censier I did everything but philosophy. This was in 1970. I tried drugs, psychoanalysis, I was ashamed of my background. But the break had come at Henri IV. I met some fellows with a lot to say for themselves, Trotskyists, that sort of thing. Socially, it was a revelation. These were highly civilised people with an advanced literary culture. I became part of that world. Later I met a whole crowd of people, real intellectuals, highly politicised. At Censier I took a year out. My mother had enrolled me at *Sciences po*.[7] That was the deal: philosophy, then *Sciences po*. So I passed the exam, I did everything I could for the sake of peace. I was leftist and feminist at *Sciences po*. One of my girlfriends was a prole. I used to dress like a leftist. I was still taking drugs. In my second year I met up with a girl who had been at Sainte Marie. We helped each other a lot. One of the sociology lecturers asked us to work with her. At 20 I was on the CNRS[8] ladder.

Despite these détours Marthe did not lose her way. She was simply 'poking her nose in elsewhere', and in so doing she learned to acknowledge her own milieu.

I moved in a particular social circle and I left it. Now I can spot them at five hundred metres. I know the way they work. I've become more tolerant nowadays. But I went through a period when I really was ashamed of my background. I'm not friendly with any of my parents' friends' friends. There are cases where transmission [of the 'culture'] goes without a hitch, but it hasn't happened with me. I had a fierce hatred of those people who simply stayed in line. I married the son of an academic from the sixteenth-district Jewish bourgeoisie. There was no relativism of knowledge at Sainte Marie, there was the well-trodden path, being keen, finding everything in the garden rosy.

Marie-Christine's grandfather was a provincial solicitor. Well informed about real estate, he had bought his children a house in the sixteenth district. Marie-Christine's parents still live there. According to Marie-Christine, they were 'a bourgeois family that did not lead a luxurious life. We were seven brothers and sisters.' They were all educated at private schools. Marie-

6 The first year of a two-year course (the second year is called *cagne*) preparing arts students for the Ecole normale supérieure, the *grande école* for the training of teachers [Tr.].

7 The Institut d'études politiques, which since 1945 has formed part of the University of Paris. Formerly the Ecole libre des sciences politiques, this college preparing students for the liberal professions and careers in public and private enterprise is still universally referred to by the old abbreviation [Tr.].

8 Centre national de la recherche scientifique, the umbrella organisation under which academic and scientific research is organised and funded nationally in France [Tr.].

Christine's parents wanted a school where 'their seven children would be well supervised'. Adopting the indigenous criteria, we can say that Marie-Christine is part of the traditional, non-wealthy bourgeoisie, the kind that does not show off. Her comments about school uniform bear this out:

There were skirts and skirts, the Pierre Cardin and the homemade. Uniform doesn't lessen the differences. There's a kind of bourgeoisie that is very careful about the way others look upon it, not wishing to give an impression of affluence. Arising out of that, there's a stifling of any interest in one's appearance. I was too susceptible to that and for a long time I didn't care about the way I looked. My jumpers were my brothers' scout sweaters dyed navy.

Now 32, Marie-Christine still seems to care little about her appearance. Like many of her friends she wears clothes that give her a sensible, restrained look. On the day of the interview she was wearing a white blouse and a pleated kilt. Her face bore little make-up and showed traces of her recent pregnancy. As we talked she kept an eye on her eldest daughter, aged 4, helping her to tackle a jigsaw puzzle with patience; she broke off to attend to her 2-year-old son's toilet-training, and she was carrying her third child, a baby of 4 months, in her arms. The modesty of her outward appearance was underlined by the serenity and self-possession that she exhibited in the situation she found herself in. Throughout the three-hour interview she nurtured her children in a way that respected their different ages, never showing irritation but guiding and governing their various childish whims (the second child's jealousy of the baby, the oldest child's desire to be mother, etc.).

Marie-Christine had started in the nursery class at Sainte Marie de Passy and stayed there until her final year, which was 1972. 'I was in the science stream. That was where they put the girls who were regarded as less mature.'

I enjoyed what we did enormously. I wasn't bored. I remember a certain depth and a genuine feeling of academic exploration. The thinking days, like the one on Marxism, for example, were tremendous.

It should be pointed out that Marie-Christine decided to be a teacher in the private sector after working in the public sector. Her opinions about the education provided by Sainte Marie reflect this.

The main difference between private and state education is that there are those who make it their business to monitor the progress of pupils at a different level from that of teaching. The *demoiselles* of the [Sainte Marie] community have a certain conception of man and of education.

Marie-Christine then talked about the 'Notices' [*avis*], which was what they called the daily morning assemblies of all the classes of a particular set. Pupils did not go straight to their classes but were first immersed in the college atmosphere: during 'Notices' girls were seated in such a way that a section A pupil inevitably found herself placed beside a section C pupil, for instance. A set mistress (who was a member of the order) led this morning ritual, checking pupils' uniforms and delivering a message that was not necessarily academic. She gave news of pupils who were absent or talked about the Lenten effort, for example. Sometimes she would give a brief address on a particular moral or religious problem. Marie-Christine saw these 'Notices' as evidence of 'a wider educational concern'. The college's 1970 move from Passy to Rueil was another example:

The *demoiselles* were tired of the families of the sixteenth district. They felt they had changed. They did not want families enrolling their daughters purely for good results. Parents also had to accept a certain moral code, a certain religious view of life.

Marie-Christine thinks she was among those who suffered least at Sainte Marie.

I believe there are some girls who had a very bad time at the college. I had a family that compensated pretty well. We discussed things a lot. Sainte Marie being an all-female environment, you find some remarkable women and some who are very bitter.

Like Marthe, Marie-Christine also experienced a desire to look around. 'My parents offered to send me to the state school [*lycée*]. But I hadn't the courage.' After her *baccalauréat* Marie-Christine studied economics at Nanterre, where she obtained a Dip. Ed. [CAPES].

I wanted to see something else. I had an enormous desire to meet some new people. To do well at Nanterre one had to be very motivated and have plenty of personal resources.

Marie-Christine feels that Sainte Marie gave her those resources: 'I learned how to work, how to take a book and extract the meat from it, how to organise my work and have a kind of thirst for it.' Marie-Christine acknowledges that she took things easy during her first year at university. However, launched by Sainte Marie, she has continued to 'look after others' by teaching adult literacy.

I received a serious religious education, but faith is not something that can be passed on. It's a personal relationship with God. At Sainte Marie they give one a serious religious culture, not a veneer. Their faith is experienced as a living thing.

## A high-quality private education

Why Sainte Marie? Investigating family memory, I had found that girls (and very often boys) had been educated at some of France's best-known private schools: La Tour, Lübeck, Dupanloud, les Oiseaux – names that symbolise more than a century of female education in the world of the élite. Sainte Marie was always spoken of as being 'in a class of its own', as representing the 'top academic level' of such institutions.

I should point out, to avoid any misunderstanding, that the Sainte Marie colleges are not 'luxury private schools for the children of the rich'. The foundation and development of these establishments show how deeply they are rooted in the debate that gripped nineteenth-century French society concerning the education of children and more particularly of girls. Within them there took shape a conception of education in the Jesuit sense of the word, as applying to the whole person. The Sainte Marie colleges offer a certain moulding of the personality considered to be in harmony with a particular religious or moral and intellectual ethic. In this respect they seemed to us, like the portraits of Laure and Florence, to constitute a sort of ideal type.

My aim here is not to write a monograph on the Sainte Marie colleges. As I have said, the impossibility of entering the premises and gaining access to records ruled out such a project. My intention is to establish a link between education received and social milieu. As we did with *bourgeois*, let us dwell for a moment on the term *collège*. No one connected with Sainte Marie will ever use the word *institution* [the usual French term for a private school]; I was actually warned against doing so. They prefer *école* or *collège*. *Institution* is rejected because according to one Sainte Marie *demoiselle* it contradicts the very principles of the education Sainte Marie provides. Sainte Marie staff seek at all points to avoid the weight of an *institution*, 'which checks the vital elements of the mind by freezing them'. So they talk about a college instead. However, the word *institution* would seem to fit the Sainte Marie colleges perfectly – if, that is, we give it the sense that Bourdieu gives it:

Having with Poincaré recalled the importance of choice of words, I think it may be useful to point out that one need only bring together the various meanings of *instituere* and *institutio* to gain the idea of an inaugural act of constitution, foundation, even invention leading by way of education to permanent dispositions, habits, and customs. (Bourdieu 1982)

Madeleine Daniélou founded the first Sainte Marie college, Sainte Marie de Neuilly, in 1913, when the period of the 'private education of young ladies' was at its creative height. The movement marked the end of an extended debate that had been going on for more than a century regarding the kind of education that should be given to women in polite society. Through its history (which has been documented by Françoise Mayeur; see Mayeur 1979) one sees the bourgeois image of woman gradually imposing itself at the expense of the aristocratic image. One name stands out above all others, that of Monseigneur Dupanloud, Bishop of Orléans.

A husband must be given a wife, a wife who knows how to stay at home, who is capable of presiding effectively over the children's education, who knows how to listen to a serious husband, hold tender and solemn converse with him, take an interest in his career, in his studies, in his work, and encourage him in an always modest yet vigorous fashion. That is the wife who will be as described in Scripture, a true companion, that is to say an aid and support in life: *socia adjutorium*. (Dupanloud 1880)

The Bishop of Orléans was the protagonist of proper training for women who belonged to the social élite. At the time he was addressing himself to the women of the aristocracy, but as Françoise Mayeur points out:

The theme of the educating mother recurs with a curiously bourgeois flavour beneath that aristocratic pen: woman, writes Dupanloud, passes on the spirit with her blood. (Mayeur 1979)

Interestingly, we shall come across very much the sort of thing that Dupanloud was saying in 1880 on the lips of the first generations of women educated at the Sainte Marie colleges.

In 1905 the state prohibited the religious orders from teaching, and the traditional educational system for girls of the Catholic bourgeoisie was dismantled. However, even within the Catholic world there were divisions. For instance, an enlightened minority rebelled against the lack of instruction among teachers in religious orders and preferred to send their children to state secondary schools, even at the risk of their losing their faith. Voices raised in favour of dismantling the teaching orders began to find a response. One of those voices belonged to Madeleine Daniélou, who went on to open a private teacher-training college with the object of furnishing girls' private education with a body of teachers whose religious and educational training equipped them to maintain a balance between faith and knowledge. Here is Madeleine Daniélou's account of what led up to the revelation of her mission:

At university I met a girl who came from a Notre-Dame convent school. She was very pious and had a statue of the Virgin in her room. One day about three months later we were attending a lecture together when she suddenly said to me: 'Madeleine, they made me read [Anatole] France and [Ernest] Renan, I no longer believe, I've got rid of the statue of the Blessed Virgin that used to be in my room.' Her words went straight to my heart. I said to myself: But there should be a place where Catholic girls could complete their higher education without such things happening. In a flash, the whole project of the work to be done came before my mind. (Taken from the *Cahiers de Neuilly* 1956–8, published by the Sainte Marie old scholars' association)

Madeleine Daniélou managed to interest the leading figures of liberal Catholicism and certain Catholic notables (members of the royalist aristocracy and the industrial upper bourgeoisie) in the project. The work of this woman and her intellectual life need to be set in the religious, social, political and philosophical context of the late nineteenth and early twentieth centuries, to which we have briefly alluded. Catholic practice (in its institutional prerogatives and through the growth of a secular morality) was about to experience a quasi-mystical revival among the aristocratic and bourgeois élites, as witness the dramatic conversion of Paul Claudel [in 1886].

In 1915 Madeleine Daniélou's appeal was 'so strongly heard and so faithfully obeyed that an apostolic community was born of it to take up and continue the work she had begun' (Léna 1981). The apostolic community in

FORUM, 12 MARCH 1988
SAINTE MARIE OLD GIRLS' ASSOCIATION

'THE MISSION OF WOMEN
IN ALL WALKS OF LIFE'

Thinking group on the subject:
Woman as 'WIFE AND MOTHER'

Report of the meeting of SATURDAY 12 DECEMBER

I Enhancing the image of woman in the home
= Availability
– Social and cultural role, outwardness, involvement in various activities
– Family role
  children, husband, elderly relations ...
  time to be devoted to the 'awkward one'
  sensitisation to the rhythms of the members of the family unit with a
  view to improving the balance
  accounts by mothers of handicapped children: key role of the mother in
  these specific cases, and contribution of the child to the quality of the
  family relationship.

II Woman's 'quality of life'
Message from Paul VI on the mission of women
– Passing on life, educating
– Bearing witness to love, generosity
  giving her time without receiving anything in return
  inner development, as opposed to activism, which is often the reflection
  of a wish to escape
  the joy of being for others rather than the race for self-realisation
– Passing on a truth different from man's
  a 'charisma' peculiar to woman

III The pitfalls
– Is there a derogatory image of woman in the home?
  stuck in a rut of household chores
  withdrawal into the family

23 Notice of meeting
Old girls are invited to attend a 'thinking day' on woman's role in society (Sainte Marie Old Girls'
Association, 1988).

question was that of Saint Francis Xavier, to which the staff of the Sainte Marie colleges (the *demoiselles*) belong. For Madeleine Daniélou, the creation of a private school where girls could cultivate their minds without losing their faith was almost a religious imperative, 'an apostolic summons to the service of the young, the passion of the Kingdom of God to be built, and the conviction that education plays a vital role in that work of construction' (Léna 1981).

As analysed in great detail by Peretz in an article on the early years of private religious secondary education for girls in Paris, it was the 'highly uninstitutionalised' nature of that education that was 'the chief feature of independent religious schooling in France between 1905 and 1959' (when compulsory contracts with the state educational authorities were introduced). The fact of being so 'highly uninstitutionalised' permanently influenced the history of these establishments.

For one thing, founders might now choose what they were going to call their school. On that choice depended the kind of public they would attract. The terms *collège* and *lycée* were both forbidden by law, so the founders of private schools could not use them. In fact, notes Peretz, 'Mlle Pimor and Mme Daniélou adopted the illegal appellations Hulst College and Sainte Marie College' (Peretz 1985). And as we have seen, so far as the latter is concerned those associated with the place rather cling to the name. It does indeed serve to distinguish Sainte Marie from the mass of minor private schools and indicates that this is a place providing an all-round education (academic and spiritual) that must be adhered to and submitted to. By selecting the word 'college', Madeleine Daniélou was implicitly controlling her future clientele.

A further consequence of the 'highly uninstitutionalised' character of private girls' schools is the importance of the foundress. The person of Madeleine Daniélou enjoys almost symbolic status in the Sainte Marie colleges. Interestingly, Madeleine Daniélou finished top of her year (1903) in the *agrégation de lettres*,[9] ten years before founding Sainte Marie de Neuilly. According to Peretz, this detail marks her out from other foundresses, most of whom in fact resumed their university courses after launching their establishments. Another interesting piece of biographical data is that Madeleine Daniélou was married to a journalist who rose to the position of mayor before becoming a member of parliament. The marriage was to produce six children. In other words, the foundress of the Sainte Marie colleges was not just highly qualified academically but was also a wife and the mother of a large family.

Since Madeleine Daniélou's death in 1956, two women have successively headed the Sainte Marie colleges, namely Mlle d'Ynglemare and Mlle d'Ussel, both members of the Saint Francis Xavier community. However, the image of the foundress continues to influence the educational aims of the staff of the

[9] The highest competitive examination for secondary-school and university arts teachers in France [Tr.].

Sainte Marie colleges, as can be seen from this piece in the April 1986 issue of the old girls' magazine (*Bulletin de l'Association des Anciennes*):

A word from Mme Daniélou:
In June 1956 Mme Daniélou addressed the leavers – God was to take her to Him the following October – and said to them, having first spoken of the already very difficult present: 'You must face the future with confidence. You are better equipped than others, by virtue of what you have been given, to find your way successfully in this *silve* you are now entering ... There is a great task to be accomplished, which is ceaselessly to rebuild this Christian world that has always triumphed over every kind of barbarism and decadence, and for which you are needed, because it is you who will be there in ten years' time, in twenty years' time, when we shall have fallen with our mission; it is you who will carry the torch, you who will take it further.'
Nearly thirty years have passed since those words were spoken. May they still resound among us; may strength from on high hearten and stimulate the countless old girls who are committed to great acts of faith, to great tasks, or who patiently, wherever they are, tell the rosary of their joys and sufferings for the Kingdom of God.

The person of Madeleine Daniélou thus embodies, for the school, the way the status of women in the world of the élite has evolved. And the generations of the young women educated by her college who are today aged 45 and over remember and talk about the exceptional character of its foundress and what they see as the equally exceptional character of her educational objective: to make available to the women of the bourgeoisie and the aristocracy a high level of academic achievement. Her work may be said to have completed the break with the nineteenth century.

Gisèle, a 48-year-old senior teacher at a state secondary school, sums up the history of Sainte Marie in almost legendary terms:

At that time [around 1913] it was unthinkable that a woman should study at an advanced level and not lose her faith. Furthermore, it was a period when girls had a veneer; she [Mme Daniélou] wanted to show that cultural standards and religion were related.

Speaking of the old girls' association, Gisèle said:

People stick together amazingly. Most old girls have married men of worth and exercise a certain influence. They are women who sometimes have big responsibilities and are active at the religious and political levels.

Christine, 47, talks not of women called to exalted destinies but of intelligent wives. Christine does not have a job; she does charitable work and gives religious instruction. At the present time many women of that generation who are not active professionally devote much of their time to parish work. Christine's remarks are curiously reminiscent of those of Monseigneur Dupanloud. Take this one, for example:

In my class, half of them have not worked because one does after all marry young and bring up the children. At Sainte Marie they [the *demoiselles*] considered that men needed intelligent wives. In this Catholic bourgeoisie, it was thought women should be educated.

There are two levels of analysis at which some account may be given of the development of the role of the bourgeois woman in French society. The first is the right to higher education; the second is woman's place in the world of work and the mother as educator.

These young women of between 32 and 34 did not talk much about their creation legend, but most of them stressed the academic qualities of Sainte Marie; the high standard [*le top-niveau*] of the establishment was a leitmotiv running through all the interviews. Here are two examples:

I became aware of the high academic standard of Sainte Marie at the time I left. When I started work I realised that 80 per cent of people could not speak French properly and had no general culture. (Colette)

One knows how to write a letter, one knows how to organise one's thoughts and write them down. (Odile)

All the young women stress their ability to 'write a letter' and 'compose a text'. The fact is that, in our society, despite the efforts of educators, mastery of these skills is still uneven and discriminatory. In bourgeois culture, great importance is attached to the art of letter-writing. The exchange of letters is still common practice; indeed, it is obligatory in certain circumstances (invitations, thank-you letters, funeral notices, etc.). One must, for example, be familiar with the codes and forms of words enabling one to indicate the appropriate degree of intimacy or distance between oneself and the person one is writing to. Knowing how to write means knowing how to present oneself and make oneself understood. This exercise is experienced as a rule of politeness. It would be interesting to know how much room such formulae take up in telephone calls. Remember that, as Mrs Pierre I, put it, 'one is tested at table and on the telephone'.

Generally speaking, all stress the positive value of 'the intellectual thing':

They have very high standards intellectually and in terms of logic. They throw out the less intelligent ones. One sees it when girls leave – either they were mischievous or they were mediocre. (Flo)

Questioned in greater detail about the significance of this 'high intellectual standard', they talk more in terms of method and the organisation of work than in terms of quality of content. Opinions differ with regard to the latter (see the accounts of Marthe and Marie-Christine earlier in this chapter). Since the introduction of compulsory contracts with the state in 1959, Catholic private schools have been obliged to stick to the official syllabus; there is room for originality only in the way that syllabus is taught, not in terms of its content.

Summing up with a broad brush what we were told about the methods used to convey the 'intellectual thing', we have: learning to study alone, discovering how to organise one's work, reading a book and getting the 'meat' out of it, drawing up a plan, learning to think, exercising a certain mental rigour and questioning what one reads. And finally: 'In the last two years [Flo's mother told us] they develop a spirit of criticism along the lines of the Jesuit principle: one becomes somebody when one is capable of criticising the education one has received.' For the younger generation, laying unqualified claim to this 'high academic standard' is a way of perpetuating the outstanding reputation of Sainte Marie. Even today, for most of these young women who have now become mothers, Sainte Marie is still a 'pinnacle' of women's education.

Having graduated, do they pursue some professional activity or do they remain at home?

In 1960 Mlle d'Ynglemare addressed a generation of women who were anxious to enter the job market. Her lecture was reprinted in a 1981 issue of the old girls' magazine, when the editors pointed out that, even if everything had changed, the lecture nevertheless gave expression to 'a profound understanding of the complementary nature of woman and man'. What she had said was this:

A normal, balanced woman is a woman of feeling. Where in this view of things do we situate the intellectual life? Precisely in the service of the feelings; for the forces of sensibility may deviate, may stray from normality . . . Intellectual effort serves to curb excess sentimentality. The life of the intellect presupposes for its part a genuine culture, which must be 'life of the spirit, turned towards others'. However, such true culture does not necessarily correspond to the collection of diplomas. Culture, real culture, in this world of technicians, may be under threat, it lies in the hands of women . . . Woman has to be put in her true place, which is to found a home. Only women pass on the faith to little children, and the process is irreplaceable.

Sainte-Marie-educated girls still speak today of the ambiguity of that education, with its enhancement of 'the intellectual thing' and the high value it places on the spiritual mission of the young wife and mother. This is why some assert that Sainte Marie encourages one to go on to higher education while others believe equally firmly that, on leaving Sainte Marie, girls will marry and have children.

Let us look at a few figures. Of fifty mothers of girls of the class of '73, twelve had or have jobs:

company manager (husband: assistant manager)
accountant (since husband's death)
secretary (husband: engineer)
picture restorer (husband: MP)
graphologist (husband: company director)
sponsorship manager for a large insurance company (UAP) (husband: general agent in the same company)
pharmacist (husband: company secretary)

painter (husband: company chairman)
journalist (husband: management consultant)
civil servant (husband: senior manager)
executive (husband: executive in a large company)
one couple in business together.

Of the fifty girls, forty-three are currently working; forty-seven obtained degrees at the end of periods of study lasting between three and six years, sometimes more. Jobs include: researcher, accountant, teacher, communications consultant, bilingual primary teacher, journalists, hospital doctors, physiotherapist, nurses, psychologist, psychomotrician, middle manager, bilingual secretary, pharmacist, occupational therapists, paediatric nurse, fraud service control director with X, petroleum engineer, press relations manager with Y, commercial engineer, management executive, company training manager, police inspector, national museum lecturer, magazine editor, product manager, management assistant, architect, advertising manager, picture restorer.

Of the seven young women not working today, only one has never worked (Pascale, a history graduate, who married a wine grower at the age of 22 and has four children); three stopped working when the third child was born, two when the second was born, and one at the birth of the first.

Of those fifty young women, thirty-four were married in church (two are divorced), five had secular weddings, five are cohabiting with men, five profess to be single. Of the thirty-nine who are married, twenty-six wed between the ages of 19 and 24; one of the thirty-nine has four children, nine have three, nineteen have 'two for the moment' (as stated explicitly in their questionnaires), six have 'one for the moment', and four have no children as yet. One of the women cohabiting has a child.

Beyond question, former pupils of the Sainte Marie colleges are highly qualified, have salaried jobs, marry and have children; they enjoy an affluent social situation. The facilities made available by material prosperity and mutual aid within families mean that most of them are able to work without losing control of the education of their children or having to let the husband's career take precedence. Some say they work not from financial necessity but because they enjoy their jobs. Grandparents and family seats are a great help, providing a system of mutual aid unknown to previous generations, who employed the services of maids, governesses or nurses. These grandparents ensure that family values are passed on, occasionally compensating for the 'physical' absence of the mother during the day.

The smallness of the sample does not permit any generalisation, and beyond these considerations of a sociological nature we must return to our initial problem, namely what is the relationship between the education provided by Sainte Marie and bourgeois culture?

# 4

## THE PARABLE OF THE TALENTS

The educational aim of the *demoiselles* of the Sainte Marie colleges appears to be to make the child aware of the place she occupies and should occupy within the human community. The values and principles that they pass on are akin to those we have found to characterise bourgeois culture: striking a balance between over-valuing the individual and diluting him or her in the community; becoming aware of one's instincts and learning to keep them in check; in short, controlling one's relationships with other people. Once again we find that these educational principles draw their meaning from a context of paradox and ambiguity.

### The 'Christian educational operation'

Before turning to our research findings, let us have a look at a couple of extracts from the writings of Marguerite Léna. They are taken from her book on the 'spirit of education', (*L'esprit de l'éducation*; 1981) and from an article by her entitled 'The Christian vocation of education' and published a year earlier in the Sainte Marie old girls' magazine (*Bulletin de l'Association des Anciennes*). Marguerite Léna is a senior teacher on the arts side at Sainte Marie de Neuilly, and quoting her work will enable us to demonstrate the existence, within the Sainte Marie colleges, of a genuine educational quest of a specific and original kind. Education is not something that is taken for granted at Sainte Marie, where tradition is constantly being re-examined and adapted to the way in which society is developing.

Christianity and the values it embodies constitute the foundation of the education provided at the Sainte Marie colleges. There bourgeois asceticism meets the principles of religion, though it is a meeting that the *demoiselles* find difficult to accept. They would never, for instance, agree with the relationship we have established here between their educational aims and the bourgeoisie. We shall be returning to this point later.

As a loyal successor of Madeleine Daniélou, Marguerite Léna duly cites the founder:

All education is spiritual; for to educate is not to train [*dresser*] but to address [*s'adresser*]; all education takes place against a background of the spoken word and freedom. Apart from that, for Madeleine Daniélou there was only conditioning of varying degrees of effectiveness and necessity but never decisive as regards what is really happening, the thing that is enacted between freedoms and in the secret heart of each. To confuse education with training was in her view to be guilty of both a misapprehension [*méprise*] and a disparagement [*mépris*] of man. (Léna 1981)

Madeleine Daniélou saw education as a form of evangelisation; Marguerite Léna sees it as a 'universal mediator of man's humanity'. At such it can only, she says, be total.

This is how there appears explicitly in education the law that implicitly governs every individual action, guiding it from the limited goals it sets itself to the universal end that in the last analysis furnishes its strictly human meaning. [*ibid.*)

The educational relationship is by its very nature one of conflict, she says, because 'it unfolds between unequal beings and is organised in terms of growth; it brings into play authority and obedience, the clash and involvement of wills'. The relationship therefore needs to pass through 'a mutual renunciation'.

To grow up, the child must renounce what it is now for the as yet hazy outline of what it will become; but no one consents willingly to being dislodged from his positions and being guided by someone else. There is always some green elysium to be abandoned, some childhood realm to be left behind. (*ibid.*)

As for the educator, he or she must renounce 'the heady experience of power' and seduction.

So there is no education without an educator, and there is always the risk of failure. The individual cannot simply be programmed; he or she may, for reasons unknown, elude the educator. In which case 'the educator is brought painfully up against the mysterious frontier of the liberty of others, which he may not transgress and which he cannot avoid'. Given these inevitable failures, Marguerite Léna criticises all philosophies of education that tend, in her words, 'to play down this dark side of the educational relationship by attributing it purely to inadequate social structures or to psychological errors capable of being remedied'.

What, then, is 'the Christian educational operation'?

The total educational operation is that which, in the history of man, collaborates in this way with God's tireless activity in calling into being what does not exist and relaunching sacred history with every child baptised, in every culture and every epoch. (*ibid.*)

Beyond or alongside the theological character of Marguerite Léna's remarks, notice how much her conception of education owes to an anthropological view of man. Hence her insistence on the point that all true education is an all-round process. This is fundamental and explains how Sainte-Marie-educated girls are able to 'recognise' one another in later life, outside the college situation. It is also the reason why it is possible to speak of Sainte

Marie as an 'institution' in the sense we were discussing earlier. At Sainte
Marie a person is 'well made' (to borrow Marguerite Léna's equation, '*éduquer*
= *bien faire l'homme*'). Everyone must learn to 'know' him or herself in order
to live in the human community. Finding one's place in the community
represented by the college is a first step, for underlying this education there is
a particular philosophical conception of 'the person'.

A choice has to be made between self-affirmation to the point of treating others with
contempt and affirmation of others, sometimes at the expense of self. A choice has to
be made between possessing or sharing, dominating or serving. Life does not choose
for us; no one escapes these alternatives, the educator least of all. So the educator is
unable simply to appeal to the natural spontaneity of the living being to provide access
to the properly human quality of life. A work of love and trust, education is the
business of man. The biological order symbolises but does not justify it. (Léna 1981)

The place to be granted to the individual is marked out by two opposite
extremes, namely collectivism (negation/dilution of the person) and hedonis-
tic individualism (hypertrophy of the self). This was what Mlle d'Ynglemare
was talking about in a lecture delivered in 1938 (and published in the old
girls' magazine in 1980 to mark the anniversary of her death):

Totalitarian governments, which leave individuals no choice in any sphere of activity
and which inform a nation in a single direction, certainly seem to prove the advocates
of education by constraint right. Many moderns take this sense of the individual too
far and on the pretext of respecting the personality seek to give youngsters free rein
not only in their activities but also as regards their instincts and feelings.

The happy medium (between two extremes) recalls the 'neithernorism'
(Roland Barthes's *ninisme*; see Barthes 1970) peculiar to definitions of the
word *bourgeoisie*.

However, it is in the name of a Christian principle that the *demoiselles* of
Sainte Marie pay so much attention to the place to be allotted to the
individual in an educational structure. No human being can be reduced to
any other; 'the Holy Spirit speaks in each one of us', whence the theory of the
call to discover and develop the gifts contained in each individual. As
numerous interviewees suggested, 'you have to go back to the parable of the
talents'. Pupils feel this interest in each one of them 'as a person' in a very
tangible way. Indeed, they all assert that there is no anonymity. Each pupil
is known, identified and located in family and social terms. Each pupil is
appreciated individually. Everything is done on a case-by-case basis. The
place allotted to the individual is echoed right down to the very organisation
of home/school relations, there being no parents' meetings as such. During
the interview that precedes each enrolment, the principal of the establishment sees what sort of family she is dealing with. She weighs up the motives
behind the application. Academic success is never, I was told, enough to get a
girl into Sainte Marie. Staff wish to provide an 'all-round education', and

families are required to let their child be taken in hand by the college in this comprehensive way.

Two examples illustrate how, at a given moment of her school career, an individual may form the object of special treatment, even to the apparent detriment of the minimal rules of collective living.

Caroline started attending Sainte Marie de Passy at nursery-school age. Everything went very well until she reached the age of 8, when she went through a disturbed phase, seemingly as a result of the birth of a baby sister. Faced with Caroline's abrupt change of attitude, a teacher (who was also a member of the order) took action:

She was an excellent primary teacher, charismatic. She understood that there was a problem, and she arranged a system for me whereby I could go to school when I wanted to. The object was not to separate me from my mother. That year she slipped me the merit prize. (Caroline)

Véronique ran into a problem higher up the school, namely incompatibility with a science teacher.

At a state school [Véronique had attended a *lycée* before switching to the Madeleine Daniélou Centre (as the Sainte Marie de Passy college was renamed when it moved to Rueil in 1970) in *seconde*, when she was 16] they would have shown no interest. I used to chatter with the girl next to me in that lesson, but the teacher only took it out on me. It's not like me to rebel but I just exploded. I went to see the set mistress: 'You won't be going to science lessons any more. That's what you want, isn't it?' I missed them for a couple of months. Afterwards things settled down again. (Véronique)

The personalised relationship between pupils and teachers inevitably leads to tensions and may sometimes give rise to 'real nightmares'. Laure, for example, could no longer stand the person who took her for French, Latin and Greek. Incidentally, this teacher (a member of the order) was 'a terror' to many other pupils as well. At the end of the *seconde* Laure had to repeat a year. In the circumstances she asked to be allowed to leave Sainte Marie, but her mother approached the principal and arranged to have her daughter transferred to a different class. Throughout that year Laure got good marks.

However, in her last year Laure had another 'incompatibility' problem with one of her teachers and was asked to repeat. Her mother approached the principal again:

Mummy went along and wept and I was reinstated. The teacher in question had made it clear that if I attended her lessons she would leave. The set mistress decided I should stop going to the lessons. (Laure)

A Sainte Marie old girl was engaged to give Laure private lessons.

## Dominique's private diary

As in all private schools (closed worlds), an interest in the individual may be accompanied by various abuses, deviations or emotional displacements.

Dominique's private diary bears this out admirably. Dominique kept a diary throughout her adolescence and the early years of her married life. The copy she let me have is the sole evidence of this practice. The volume covers the period February–May 1956, when Dominique was *en première* at Sainte Marie de Neuilly, aged 16.

Day by day, over 250 pages, Dominique records her thoughts and feelings. She writes about what happens to her at college with her friends and the teachers. The family takes up only a very small amount of space. She devotes some fifty pages to the Easter holidays, which she spent at Porquerolles [in the Iles d'Hyères, off Toulon]. It was a time of freedom. Dominique was then 'in the middle of an adolescent crisis'. The diary is larded with moral quotations; Dominique copied out prayers, poems and extracts from novels as well as writing poetry herself. Every day there is a comment on academic endeavours and intellectual tensions. But the core of the diary is the fierce battle waged by Dominique to assert her personality in the face of the institution, as embodied by her set mistress. To gain the set mistress's attention, Dominique says she does not believe in God.

But let us look at some extracts:

1 March 1956
> First day of exams.
> Singing rehearsal.
>
> 'Lord Jesus, teach me to be generous
> To serve you as you deserve
> To give and not to count the cost
> To fight and not to heed the wounds
> To toil and not to seek for rest
> To work and not to look for any reward save that of knowing that I do your holy
>      will'.                                                        (Saint Ignatius)

... French essay: choose about ten lines of poetry that you like and attempt to distinguish what constitutes their magic.

3 March
> Got 14 for my dogma composition despite the idiotic things I came out with. Detachment: not through renunciation but freedom of mind in relation to what is not God. Detachment from this world = attachment to J.C., not negative but positive.
> Philosophy essay: the scientist discovers, the artist creates.

6 March
> Sick, sick, sick of life. Disgusting feebleness. No rebellion: haven't the strength. Loneliness, resigned despair, but
> I don't give a damn
> Don't give a don't give a don't give a damn
> Piss off
> Shit
> Those are my litanies and prayers for the moment. Having said which, let's not go overboard: this is a temporary irritation.
> French essay now marked.

Poetry: not richness in itself but in what it evokes (Annie); a foretaste of the good to which all men aspire (Marie-France, who came top with 15).

Wednesday 7 March
[Dominique writes an imaginary letter to d'A. (her set mistress). She pictures herself at Porquerolles. In the letter she reveals her suffering and reproaches the set mistress for not helping her.]
I hate d'A. all the more for having loved her. Oh I can admit it, I love her. Why hide the fact? Does Chantal F. hide it? No, and she's not as ridiculous as Jeanne or Chantal E., who refuses to admit it.

Sunday 8 March
Snowed under with work.
Utterly fed up, I've had it up to here. I've spent 6 hours on the central plateau and haven't finished it, and anyway, what do I know about it?
Shall I survive till Tuesday evening?
I'm in a completely false situation. I've chucked religion but that doesn't chime with my vocation.
Appalling nervous exhaustion.
Sick, sick, sick.

Monday 12 March
Geog. essay tomorrow.
Tomorrow it will all be over . . .
Phew.
But I'm tired, I'm thinking not about the holidays but about the third term. They're so short, it's so long. And the exams at the end of it, they really terrify me.
But let's not anticipate.
I'm well aware that I'm only a poor, stupid, detestable cretin who doesn't deserve any attention, and even when someone does pay her some attention shouldn't believe in it: d'A., for instance, was super when I was ill.
Of course, I wasn't so stupid as to believe it was for me personally but for me as a member of the class; I know now it was just sense of duty.

Next day
M.-F. is depressed and unable to shake it off by herself.
She finds that humiliating.
C. is depressed and tries to hide the fact. She doesn't want to be a nuisance to others.
There are some things one should never touch because they're sacred. I.e. everything described as personal.

Friday 16
Translation in class.
At half past six, conversation with C. [a friend]. I told her that I don't wish to make my Easter communion and that I no longer want to practise my religion. She was alarmed and told me to read Pascal's wager. She doesn't look much but she's amazing. I cannot be a saint, that I must accept. C. is going to speak to d'A. Only I have no illusions: either she won't take me seriously or she will despise me and she'll be right. Only that is not how she's going to convert me.
I can hear d'A. telling me: 'So for a few miserable set-backs of a purely sentimental, subjective nature you throw over everything!' (withering scorn).
I wish I could stop thinking about it all, but it obsesses me.

Saturday 17 March

At half past twelve I found myself alone with d'A., who told me I'd been 'sombre and silent recently' and asked me whether it was on account of work or whether this was 'the time of deep thoughts'; she'd hit both nails on the head, but I said nothing in reply; anyway, she teased me so sweetly I found myself laughing along with her. But I stayed on the defensive, not trusting her winning ways: I won't be caught out again. It may cost me to stand up to her but I must.

If d'A. summons me, I'll keep my mouth shut because words traduce and misrepresent thought.

If d'A. summons me, I mustn't fly off the handle and I mustn't have any illusions!

If d'A. summons me, it'll be more from duty than from love, a tiresome duty and one where you feel she'd rather be doing something else.

Monday 19 March

This evening d'A. spoke to me, she was very nice. *Watch out.*

She told me to send her a sketch from Porquerolles.

Wednesday 21 March

Translation in class; aches from gym, depression.

I leave in a week but not for long ... [there follow three long pages on Dominique's feelings for d'A.: 'She doesn't like me, she likes the others.'].

Friday 23 March

It's the holidays and that gives me no pleasure at all. C. has spoken to d'A, who said she knew: she said it was normal, it would pass, it was normal with artists. It makes me furious that she doesn't take me seriously, and what makes me especially furious is that she's right, that she doesn't wonder about me at all, and that she casually files me away among matters already settled in advance. Well, if she thinks I'm going to come back to God so easily, she's left a big factor out of account – my pride!

Saturday 24 March

Yesterday afternoon I was wretchedly bored and slept like a dormouse. Parents horrified: 'That's all we need – her ill when we're leaving!' Woke up in time to go and see *Bread, Love, Amen* [*Pain, amour, ainsi soit-il* – a play, possibly]: utterly stupid. Dinner afterwards at the Brasserie Alsacienne in the Champs-Elysées. In my navy skirt fastened with a safety pin, I was the picture of the little convent schoolgirl. So what, I don't care.

Dominique continues her diary with an account of her holidays at Porquerolles (amorous adventures with a sailor and 'some kitchen boys'; Dominique talks of a 'change of milieu'). She is happy. Then it is back to Sainte Marie: several poems, various remarks about 'Notices', and comments on a French teacher's lessons, books she is reading, music, and so on.

Relations between Dominique and d'A. continued as follows:

I went to ask d'A. for some maps for the charity sale. She took the opportunity to deliver a well-intentioned little homily on 'my great gifts' (???), saying how one must opt for a noble cause. She says she knows me well. I wonder how true that is. At any rate, she's guessed that I have not yet opted for or against a noble cause. In fact I've opted against, though it cannot be said that my cause is contemptible. I must choose between sanctity (or heroism) and good sense. I go for good sense. Very sensible. She talked about her brother, who was killed in Algeria. I admire her. She spoke of him with such simplicity, not snivelling at all, in admiration and faith. 'It's extraordinary to think that now he has seen God.' What I admire is more her guts than her faith, in fact; more her way of seeing her faith than her faith for its own sake.

She claims I have improved latterly. I'd like to think so but don't feel I've changed all that much in a fortnight!

She showed me some newspaper cuttings mentioning her brother. I'm pleased to have been taken into her confidence like that, introduced to her family, as it were, and to her inmost feelings. She is terrific, it has to be said. She told me one must have a goal that one follows without ever swerving from one's path. Maybe. But it does mean one is blinkered rather, one passes the beautiful things in life by without seeing them. I prefer Montaigne's anti-systematic approach, taking things as they come, as and when, sufficient unto the day, etc. *Carpe diem.*

## The *demoiselles* and bourgeois culture

By refusing to attach too much importance to 'states of mind' but nevertheless respecting the individual, the staff of the Sainte Marie colleges teach girls to find their own place, providing principles and structures to guide them.

There is nothing particularly original about the principles. They are directly descended from the civilities propounded by Erasmus, while drawing their educational inspiration from Jesuit thought. Principle number 1 is to control the child's instincts. Mlle d'Ynglemare again:

First of all, children must be made to understand that the usages required by politeness are after all merely indicative of a high degree of civilisation . . . The child first learns of its own accord to curb its appetites and to restrain excessive and vulgar manifestations of the emotions: loud laughter, shouting, floods of tears, uncoordinated movements, excitement, thoughtless utterances . . . Then it makes its first attempts at being sociable, which means in the first place learning to avoid what may upset other people, then training itself to practise courtesy in its relationships, correctness in its use of language, maximum sophistication in the expression of thought, freedom in its behaviour, and the kind of amiable simplicity that is the height of distinction.

It is not difficult to draw a comparison between such educational principles and 'bourgeois culture', and we shall see how the *demoiselles* of Sainte Marie do indeed combat the 'snobbery or display of wealth' to which girls who are 'not yet educated' easily succumb.

One way of controlling children's impulses and instincts is to restrain 'excessive friendships' by separating girls who are 'too friendly' with each other. Such bonds may generate passionate feelings that then permit the child to duck authority and disrupt a class. A number of girls were separated from friends in this way. Laure C. was summoned by the set mistress to be told she was to stop going around with two friends who 'talked nonsense' and were apparently having a bad influence on her. Laure C. ignored the advice, considering it 'appallingly petty and thoroughly stupid'. Chantal reacted differently: she followed the recommendations of the set mistress and lost a friend.

I had a friend in the sixth class but the following year the sister called me in to tell me she was not the right sort of friend for me. We were not from the same milieu. Her father was bourgeois but her mother was of artisan stock. The grandfather was illiterate. My parents didn't like her: she was happy, independent.

The closed system of the college offers a rich breeding ground for close friendships, so these are carefully monitored. However, Chantal's case goes beyond the mere question of over-intense relationships, raising that of the appreciation of social or cultural differences. Part of educating a girl is teaching her how to recognise her own kind. From childhood a person is taught to keep emotional impulses within reasonable bounds and to understand that unbridled romantic feelings do not necessarily lead to happiness. One should never let oneself go: it represents a loss of autonomy and a waste of energy. In concrete terms, should Chantal wish to invite this close friend to a ball, she would have to face the possibility of a refusal and thus put herself in a situation that would be difficult not just for her but also for her friend. Better to take avoiding action.

In order to control the child's instincts, stress is laid on 'the intellectual aspect' and an attempt is made to channel pupils' enthusiasms in the direction of developing their talents.

'What do you see as the principal quality of the teaching given at Sainte Marie?' we asked these young women in our questionnaire. They all put things like: 'Chiefly the intellectual standard, the quality of the teachers, the schooling in intellectual rigour', and so on.

Everyone agreed that it was not a good thing, at Sainte Marie, to be a bad pupil. For some, life was dominated by fear and humiliation. Caroline, who was a very good pupil, conceded that

It is a system that operates on fear. You're not punished if you do something wrong, you're punished before. It's a case, perhaps, of preventive repression. We were extraordinarily obedient pupils. You could have the feeling of having done something wrong without having done anything. You based your conduct on what was expected of you.

The aim was intellectual homogeneity. Girls of whom it was said that 'Sainte Marie does not suit them' were expelled. They disappeared, directed towards schools with a less exalted academic reputation. Girls accepted such practices without rebelling. Marie-Christine, for example, found nothing odd about seeing one of her sisters leave Sainte Marie 'because she was not interested in things of the mind'. Another acknowledged 'with no feeling of rebellion' that she had stayed on at Sainte Marie despite her 'very average standard'. Her mother interceded with the principal regularly. Danièle, aged 50, said:

My sister got herself thrown out in her final year on the grounds that she was poor at Latin. The teachers thought she wouldn't pass her school-leaving exam. She did, but at another school. My other sister wasn't gifted academically. She was told she would blossom elsewhere.

Some years later Danièle sent her own daughters to Sainte Marie de Neuilly. The eldest worked hard and behaved well until the *seconde*, when she was three times disciplined for absconding. Danièle was then called in: 'Your daughter B. is not happy with us, she would be much better off somewhere else.' Danièle took the advice. A few years later she sent her second daughter to Sainte Marie. The second daughter was well-behaved but came bottom of the class. Her mother was summoned:

'If your daughter [now aged 11] dropped Latin she could concentrate more on French and maths.' Since Latin is all they do at Sainte Marie, that meant expulsion. But I knew the background and I was not surprised at them getting rid of my daughters. I did something with some student teachers that I shouldn't have done.

At all events, in the name of respect for the individual, Colette, a former Sainte Marie pupil, now a member of the old girls' association and a highly qualified teacher who has chosen to practise her profession in the state sector (seeing it as her Christian duty), was prompted to say without demagogy but without fear of being thought élitist: 'They [the *demoiselles*] are trying to produce intelligent Christian people. They don't keep children who are not gifted.' A similar statement was made by a teacher at the Madeleine Daniélou Centre:

We had a little girl in the fifth class [Year 8] who was giving us a bit of a headache. It was her background ... She lived in Rueil, and her mother had led a somewhat stormy existence. She was a very charming little girl ... She already thought about nothing but boys and always criticised what one did. Her voice could be heard in the dining-hall, at break, or in the corridors between lessons. She started smoking. If we expelled her, she'd have no chance. But the sister said 'If we keep her in school, ten or a dozen will have no chance.' The harder you try, the more the child gets out of her depth. It's better she should be in a school environment that suits her. Because this is a very rich education where one is stretching pupils as much as one can.

So it is in the name of respect for the individual that the Sainte Marie colleges have developed and justify a certain élitism. The parable of the talents, so often mentioned during interviews, lends 'official' legitimacy to the process by serving as a point of reference that is beyond discussion. But what does the parable of the talents actually say?

It is like a man going abroad, who called his servants and put his capital in their hands; to one he gave five bags of gold, to another two, to another one, each according to his capacity. Then he left the country. The man who had the five bags went at once and employed them in business, and made a profit of five bags, and the man who had the two bags made two. But the man who had been given one bag of gold went off and dug a hole in the ground, and hid his master's money. A long time afterwards their master returned, and proceeded to settle accounts with them. The man who had been given the five bags of gold came and produced the five he had made: 'Master', he said, 'you left five bags with me; look, I have made five more.' 'Well done, my good and trusty servant!' said the master. 'You have proved trustworthy in a small way; I will now put you in charge of something big. Come and share your master's delight.' The man with the two bags then came and said, 'Master, you left two bags with me; look, I have made two more.' 'Well done, my good and trusty servant!' said the master. 'You have proved trustworthy in a small way; I will now put you in charge of something big. Come and share your master's delight.' Then the man who had been given one bag came and said, 'Master, I knew you to be a hard man: you reap where you have not sown, you gather where you have not scattered; so I was afraid, and I went and hid your gold in the ground. Here it is – you have what belongs to you.' 'You lazy rascal!' said the master. 'You knew that I reap where I have not sown, and gather where I have not scattered? Then you ought to have put my money on deposit, and on my return I should have got it back with interest. Take the bag of gold from him, and give it to the one with the ten bags. For the man who has will always be given more, till he has enough and to spare; and the man who has not will forfeit even what he has. Fling the useless servant out into the dark, the place of wailing and grinding of teeth!' (Matthew 25: 14–30 NEB)

Reading this text, it is impossible not to be struck by the harshness of the message: 'For the man who has will always be given more, till he has enough and to spare; and the man who has not will forfeit even what he has.' That the parable should be capable of inspiring the 'Christian educational operation' is even more intriguing. Let us not stray too far down the paths of exegesis but stay within the parable's context of use and usage. A parable is first of all a manner of speaking. When the disciples ask him, 'Why do you speak to them in parables?' Jesus replies:

It has been granted to you to know the secrets of the Kingdom of Heaven; but to those others it has not been granted. *For the man who has will be given more, till he has enough and to spare; and the man who has not will forfeit even what he has.* That is why I speak to them in parables; for they look without seeing, and listen without hearing or understanding. (Matthew 13: 11–13 NEB)

God's word needs to be heard and received. To propagate it, Jesus addresses those who 'look without seeing and listen without hearing' in the clear, living language of the parable. In the explanation given for this mode of discourse we find the same discriminatory assertion as was used in the parable of the talents. According to the official French Roman Catholic commentary, Jesus is taking issue in this passage with the religious leaders of his day. God's word has been entrusted to them, and they have hoarded it. But it is a living force, God's word, not a dead letter. The man who has (received it) must grow and increase (the servant and his 'talents' or bags of gold).

So the parable of the talents sets out the need for apostolic activity. People are not to wait for the Kingdom of God without doing anything. 'Faith [says the commentary] is not an easy guarantee exempting a person from facing up to life but a demand for growth and action.'

The *demoiselles* of Sainte Marie, guided by Jesuit thought, make education into an apostolic activity. This conception carries with it its own dialectic: the pupil who has (received) must increase and give; that is what 'having the Sainte Marie spirit' means. Silent retreats, for example, enable girls to receive a deeper religious education but also to get to know themselves. And while self-knowledge leads to God, it also leads to obedience to what one is, an obedience that is willing, considered and deliberate. This is the very heart of Saint Ignatius's *perinde ac cadaver*, 'to obey like a corpse'.

These theological underpinnings enable the *demoiselles* of Sainte Marie not to burden themselves with pupils who may balk their instructors. The institution picks out those who do not fit into the system. Remember Marguerite Léna's remarks on philosophies of education that invariably seek, every time and at all costs, to explain academic failure in rational terms. Her criticisms are inspired by the general principle that there exists in every human being an element of irreducible mystery. The conception of education entertained by the *demoiselles* of Sainte Marie cannot be reduced to élitism pure and simple. Indeed, in one and the same family one child is kept on while her sister is expelled. It really is the individual person that is at issue here. The child learns a certain severity, firstly with regard to itself in that it must learn to evaluate its own potential very precisely. At the very least, the system may be said to be innocent of demagogy. This is how it helps to inculcate the 'self-control' and asceticism that characterise bourgeois culture.

## Others

Its instincts once controlled and channelled towards kindling its intelligence and developing its intellectual skills, the child learns to live in the community. Structures are put in place to create this balance between self and others – 'others' meaning first and foremost the college.

The set mistresses (all members of the Saint Francis Xavier community) serve to create what our informants have referred to as 'the college spirit'. They may be teachers, but their primary function is to provide religious instruction and to co-ordinate the forms of a particular level. They keep an eye on relations between pupils, staff and college. We have already come across them several times, performing their function in concrete terms. We have seen, for example, how each morning they take the assemblies known as *avis*. As soon as the girls arrive in school they make their way to a room where all the forms of a particular year meet. The seating arrangements ensure that girls always find themselves sitting next to members of other forms. The set mistress is responsible for what happens during these assemblies, which last about half an hour. She will speak on a particular topic concerning the life of the college (voluntary work, the Lenten effort) or give news of any girls who are sick or absent. But she may also tackle a broader issue and embark, for example, on a religious exercise. She will also inspect dress, spotting any infringements of the rules. It is a solemn moment, when the individual is immersed in the group, a daily ritual aimed at creating a feeling of belonging to a group. It symbolises the passage from individual to collective, providing a balance between the attention devoted to each pupil and 'the college spirit'.

The feeling of belonging to the college is also nourished by various activities made available to the pupils as a body. These include retreats linked to religious observance, when all the girls go away together for two or three days' meditation and prayer, trips organised by the *demoiselles* to Rome, Spain or elsewhere, dramatic productions, the Lenten effort, and so on.

All this is reminiscent of the typical organisation of Jesuit colleges (as documented in Chartier, Compère and Julia 1976). 'Having the college spirit' means joining in these various activities enthusiastically. The concern to provide an all-round education can also be seen in the opportunities for voluntary work offered to Sainte Marie girls. This 'openness to others' is seen as an 'openness to the outside world'.

It's not a doctrine they pass on but a personal strength. They develop one's personal qualities. The power of the Ignatian view of the world is not necessarily a bad thing. There is a good way and a bad way of exercising it, namely as power for oneself or as service to others. Not assuming one's responsibilities is a way of not regarding others as valid partners. (Marie-Christine)

First the child, then the adolescent, caught up in a system in which she is both valued as an individual and immersed in a 'college spirit', is thus also expected to 'open out towards others': to grow and increase.

There is a paradox here. In answer to the question: 'What in your view is the principal quality of the education provided at Sainte Marie?' people cited, as we have seen, in the first place its intellectual quality and in the second its moral quality: 'one learns to respect others, open out towards others'. In answer to the question: 'What in your view is the principal defect of the education provided at Sainte Marie?' we were told variously 'lack of openness', 'an over-protected milieu despite an apparent openness to the outside world', 'sectarianism', 'élitism', 'education insufficiently open towards the outside world' (see appendix for the other replies given to these questions).

Openness and enclosedness: as a matter of principle, the Sainte Marie colleges are open to all, regardless of social standing or religion; they are multi-denominational, with Catholics forming the majority. All they do, the *demoiselles* claim, is guarantee a high standard of academic teaching and a moral education inspired and guided by Christian principles. Several facts aim to transform this principle into reality:

1 The relatively low fees (adjusted in accordance with parental income and number of children).
2 The foundation of the Charles Péguy[1] schools, so-called, according to the foundress of one of the earliest of them, 'because of all that that name

---

[1] Charles Péguy (1873–1914), socialist turned mystical Catholic essayist and poet who died in action at the Battle of the Marne [Tr.].

symbolises in terms of deep Christian meaning and true love of the popular soul'.

The foundation around 1933 of the Charles Péguy schools, conceived initially as district primary schools, formed part of a wider missionary thrust aimed at the suburban working class. Schools were set up at Courbevoie, La République, Bobigny, Montreuil and Rueil. Gradually these Charles Péguy primary schools turned into private schools. The Courbevoie school moved to Rueil in 1968, 'drawn by the large blocks of council flats forming the La Fouilleuse estate'. The school at La République, founded in 1941, was rather different from its suburban counterparts. It took in (and still takes in) children and young people from very different social, cultural, philosophical and religious backgrounds: children of artisans, tradesmen, industrialists, managers; nowadays the school is also open to foreigners, the eleventh district being the part of Paris that has more of them than any other.

3 The foundation of Sainte Marie colleges in Africa.

A telephone conversation with a senior member of staff at Sainte Marie de Neuilly made clear that, to the *demoiselles*, the problem of social openness remains a fundamental concern. Indeed, their Christian vocation cannot encompass the idea that they are, in practice, the educators of privileged milieux alone. This is despite the fact that Madeleine Daniélou's original project chimed with the preoccupations of a certain section of the Catholic upper bourgeoisie and aristocracy.

The limits of this investigation (a single year group of girls from the Sainte Marie de Passy college, the last two years of whose schooling had been at the new location of the college, renamed the Madeleine Daniélou Centre, in Rueil, and other women educated at Sainte Marie de Neuilly) make it impossible to generalise. On the contrary, prudence is very much in order here, since the evidence supplies contrasting opinions.

Before Rueil there were social differences but one was not aware of them. The education was the same. After Rueil, I found that that had changed. They told us: 'We're going to open out.' Basically they'd changed nothing, except that at the level of tradition things were in fact different, it wasn't the same families any more, it was the new rich. (Laure)

On the other hand Christiane, who was in the same year as Laure, felt that the move to Rueil had not really altered the social level of the college's intake. However, she said, 'my sister, who started in the first year at Rueil, says they did succeed in opening the place up. There was a whole population that didn't belong to the bourgeoisie.'

Sandrine, also from the same year group, said:

At Rueil, new girls arrived: they had a different way of speaking from us. I think they used words that bordered on vulgarity. We had been corrected since very early childhood.

Finally, the comments of a lay teacher at the Madeleine Daniélou Centre:

The principal of the Daniélou Centre wanted, by moving to Rueil, to open up to other social circles. She thought she could draw on Nanterre and the suburbs. She was very disappointed. It was mainly families of high-level technicians who had two children and no more. They lacked generosity. Generosity means giving one's time to something for free. Girls from Charles Péguy schools are automatically taken into the seventh at Daniélou, when they're often closer to the fifth [i.e. very advanced for their age]. Those girls whose parents were high-level technicians were high-powered but blinkered. That's precisely where they needed educating. They didn't take sides but they never volunteered for extra-curricular activities. A person needs a certain spirit. You've been given certain talents, you don't make fun of other people, you have to make those talents bear fruit for them. If you live for yourself, you dry up.

Since we cannot provide a systematic analysis of the sociological profile of Sainte Marie pupils, let us confine ourselves to looking at the professions of the fathers of the girls of the class of '73. We find:

2 senior executives in large companies
1 high-ranking civil servant working under the President of the National Assembly
1 company manager
9 engineers
1 technician
2 sales managers
1 inspector of taxes
1 member of parliament
1 industrialist
1 architect
1 management auditor
1 shopkeeper
1 representative
1 wine grower
1 company organiser
8 company directors (4 chairmen)
1 printer
1 government minister
1 insurance agent
1 banker
1 naval officer
1 doctor
2 lawyers
1 director of the Bank of France
1 stockbroker

The first thing to note is that the upper classes dominate and no manual occupations are represented. Anonymity forbids me from supplying proof that we are indeed dealing here with the bourgeoisie and the aristocracy. And if such were not the case, why should the *demoiselles* of Sainte Marie put so much effort into combating the outward signs of wealth and the idleness that social affluence can engender?

They never stop telling you: you belong to a materially privileged section of society. They spit on you every morning. Apart from that, we were the intellectual élite. (Louise)

You were taught that you were from a well-to-do milieu but that you must behave in such a way that it didn't show. (Caroline)

The teachers had an obsession about snobbery. It's not because of this or that that you are better than others. On the other hand, since one is better than the rest, having the chance to receive such an education, it would be a crime not to improve yourself. (Flo)

They won't have any kind of class spirit; advancement, that sort of thing. They try to open people up to generosity: Little Sisters of the Poor, charity work, child adoption. They don't content themselves with facilitating reproduction of the bourgeois model. (Colette)

Uniform may seem an anachronism today, but it does serve to conceal differences, combat clothing excesses and enable 'any poor girls' to avoid suffering from inequality. Brigitte, whose father's family were traditionally butchers from father to son (a wholly relative poverty, in other words), admits to having agreed to start at the Madeleine Daniélou Centre in 1970 because they wore uniform ('if it hadn't been for that, I'd never have gone there'). All agreed, however, that the uniform conceals nothing and that girls learn to decipher the tiny details indicating the differences that exist between them. What the uniform actually does is to symbolise membership of a group, to place 'college' apart from the motley of everyday existence.

What is it that constitutes 'openness to others'? Beyond a declared but not necessarily implemented intention of being open to all sections of society, Sainte Marie seeks to steer the child towards others, the 'others' in question being destitute families, the handicapped, the sick, the blind, old ladies, and so on.

Most of the girls valued these extra-curricular activities. Laure C. left Sainte Marie for a year to attend a state school; the strict supervision, the tyrannical power of certain set mistresses and the social isolation still strike her as intolerable today. Nevertheless, she may send her own daughter to Sainte Marie de Neuilly 'because included in the timetable were activities for others, reading to the blind or going to Garches to look after handicapped children'. Herself now an adult and responsible for bringing up a daughter, Laure C. will do her duty in providing her ('at the age when that sort of thing makes an impression') with opportunities to acquire 'the sense of giving'.

For Odile, religion was not a factor, 'the ethical question was far more present':

We used to save up during Lent. Collecting boxes were handed out, and at the end of Lent all the money was given to charity [specifically, '*Frères des Hommes*']. You could attend catechism classes with the disadvantaged in Saint-Cloud, be a stretcher-bearer at Lourdes. There was no compulsion. They wanted to confront us with other milieux. (Odile)

A big board was put up at the beginning of the year, suggesting various voluntary activities. Every girl put her name down where she wished. It is true there was no compulsion, but we know the report card had three columns: work, individual conduct and group conduct.

This openness to others does not in fact impinge on the social world. Privileged children are being taught to be sensitive to other people's misfortunes. The relationship remains a personal one; it is a question of one individual getting to grips with another individual. Such a way of experiencing others through voluntary acts of generosity allows these women not to think of 'social inequality' in terms of conflict. Inequality, for them, will be one of the constituents of reality (just like the variety of gifts present within each individual). Everyone can do his or her bit towards remedying human misfortune. 'We are deeply moral people: we are very sensitive to others' (Flo). These girls are able to say in the same breath that Sainte Marie is not open towards the outside world and that Sainte Marie teaches openness to others.

It is impossible not to say something about the countless reflections on the feeling of confinement experienced by these girls during their time at school. Marthe and Marie-Christine, extracts from whose interviews were reproduced in chapter 3, voiced something that virtually all the young women interviewed felt and in some cases denóunced. However, the feeling stemmed as much from the ubiquity of the 'milieu' as from the school itself. It was the close link between attending Sainte Marie and the family and/or the social traditions of a section of the bourgeoisie that produced such a sense of being 'shut in'.

There was one road to cross. If it hadn't been Sainte Marie, it would have been La Tour or Lübeck [other private schools in Paris]. Had to be: it goes with the milieu. (Odile)

My mother knew Sainte Marie was a good school. The choice of a church school didn't pose any problems. My sister had gone there at the age of ten, I started in the nursery class, my brother went to Franklin. (Caroline)

Whether from family tradition or environmental influence, sending one's daughters to one of the Sainte Marie colleges is something that is taken for granted. No one questions it. Most of the parents of those interviewed had themselves gone to private schools. Their brothers had gone to Franklin, Saint Jean de Béthune, Gerson, Sainte Croix de Neuilly, and so on.

One cannot compare oneself to others. One was very shut in. I didn't know anyone who went to a state school [lycée]. Some girls may have been able in their final years to meet other young people at parties but not me. When I took my school-leaving exam was the first time I'd set foot inside a state school. We were told we would be victimised by the examiners. Going inside a state school meant risking damnation, all the teachers were atheist, Communists, Marxists. (Caroline)

In the senior classes some girls tried to get away. 'When I was at Sainte Marie', Laure C. told me, 'that was all I knew. The home–school round trip and that was it.' Laure asked for and was granted permission to go to the Lycée Molière when she was 16.

My mother said nothing. When I started at the state school it was like discovering Paris, we used to go out so much. I went to cafés, started smoking, discovered life, you know? I was lucky to do so when I did because afterwards, at university, you can get thrown out. At Sainte Marie I had a very strong sensation of not being able to breathe any more. At the state school I was taking it so easy that I decided to return to Sainte Marie to take my school-leaving exam.

Lorraine, too, had only one wish: to escape. But she had to wait until she had finished school.

After Sainte Marie I did a year at *catho*[2] to go on to the Sorbonne. Living in the eighth district, I should have gone to Nanterre. I did English without taking my degree. I had an impression of extraordinary freedom: I spent three years running wild. I really wanted to escape from my milieu: one wasn't like other people. One had the same cast of mind, the same style of dressing, the lot, you know?

Imprisoned in Sainte Marie and in their social milieu, these girls were acutely alive to the apparent heterogeneity of their world. Here we can return to the accounts given by Marthe and Marie-Christine. The latter particularly remembers that at weekends she was very badly dressed. 'The other girls used to dress up like anything. In my family we were taught that you belonged to a well-to-do milieu but that you must behave in such a way that it didn't show.' Caroline drew a distinction between Catholic families, with lots of children and houses falling into ruin, families that had launched themselves into Parisian society and aristocrats. 'A very powerful differentiation is not having a handle to your name. I took that very badly. It's a question of class antiquity.' Geneviève, a member of the aristocracy, said that 'money and social position were respected'. One quickly learned to do the done thing.

I had a friend who lived in my street. She wasn't from the same milieu. Her father had a good job, an X [as graduates of the Ecole Polytechnique are familiarly called], but wasn't well-connected. An intelligent fellow, my mother used to say. I really liked that girl. I used to see her in certain circumstances. But I very soon made distinctions. The tennis set was not the same as the pontoon set.[3] I used to take that girl along with me to the tennis set. At balls I didn't mix. None of this posed any problems for me.

This sensitivity with regard to detecting one's peers, coupled with a recognition of differences without treating those differences as distinctions,

---

[2] Institut catholique de Paris, a Catholic theological college.
[3] The reference is to a certain landing-stage on the Lake of Annecy that formed one of the social landmarks in the lives of holidaying young bourgeois.

allowed many of these young women to think they were capable of 'mixing with all sorts'. The illusion is permissible, it has to be said, in the case of those with the longest pedigree in the bourgeois world.

One was aware of differences when one visited people, there's the swish split-level apartment in Neuilly and there's the three-roomed flat. My daughter was friendly with a girl whose father was a taxi-driver. My daughters have friends from all milieux. Those from less privileged backgrounds reckon they had a bad time at Sainte Marie, but that was their fault, they drew comparisons, it didn't come from the others. (Danièle)

These young women of thirty still remember a feeling of confinement. Some of them cannot stand navy blue. Others refuse to believe in God. Most got married in church, in many instances to a man from the same milieu ('give or take the odd nuance'), and those who have had children all want to pass on to them what they consider to be an essential value, namely generosity or the sense of giving.

Christian principles and Jesuit influence underlie the educational aims of the *demoiselles* of Sainte Marie. The teaching and practice of religion are fully integrated in the curriculum, where they are regarded as 'intellectual facts' giving access to 'the life of the spirit'. It is a permanent impregnation giving structure to the personality: self-knowledge with a view to controlling impulses; the learning of intellectual rigour and personal modesty; a battle against boastfulness of any kind; the feeling of belonging to 'a class' vanishing beneath the concept of generosity, because openness towards others creates the profound yet ambiguous illusion that anyone can acquire these values provided she has the right 'talent'.

In the light of the parallel we have drawn between bourgeois culture and 'the Christian educational operation', it is impossible not to draw a further parallel between the Jesuit colleges of the eighteenth century and the Sainte Marie colleges of today. The principal postulate of Jesuit educational thinking was egalitarian. However, as Chartier, Compère and Julia point out in their 1976 study of education in France from the sixteenth to the eighteenth centuries, whereas in the eighteenth century pupils were regarded as equal for the purpose of religious exercises, 'society took care to set things straight again'. Avowed principles notwithstanding, inequalities of status and wealth were reflected in the numbers who quit in that they made certain people 'unsuited' to the system. However, the phenomenon was one of complementarity rather than contradiction. 'It was the more popular strata of recruitment that supplied both the principal victims of the selection process and the most brilliant students academically' because it was precisely they who illustrated the validity of the egalitarian postulate. *It was a question of the individual, not of class.* Merit, hard work, discipline and 'considered, voluntary, deliberate obedience' enabled those who exhibit them to hold their own. It is just as if, so far as the staff of Sainte Marie are concerned, school were not compulsory. Anyone and everyone is free to send their daughters to Sainte Marie; Sainte Marie is free to decide who is and is not suited to its system. There are many other places that are less exigent, where the desire to provide an all-round education does not dominate and the child is left with whole areas of its personality that are not under the control of the institution.

The *demoiselles* of Sainte Marie are thus unable to accept that they are educators of the well-to-do classes alone. Yet their educational aims correspond to the basic expectations of such families. In the 1970s Groethuysen asked whether the Church was about to give its blessing to the bourgeoisie (Groethuysen 1977). The bourgeoisie, whether believing or non-believing, has not waited for an answer.

It has made 'the Christian virtues' its own by secularising them.

# 5

## THE THREE GENERATIONS

So one learns to become bourgeois as one learns to have taste (Gadamer, quoted in Habermas 1989). And to that end one must occasionally renounce oneself and one's personal preferences. As in law, the imposition of a duty may conflict with an individual's private inclinations. That duty must become second nature. Hence the peculiar difficulty we encounter when seeking to disentangle and understand what is put forward as self-evident, because those who conform to such behaviour have a special kind of awareness of it: they see it as integral to a world view – one, moreover, that they imagine to be universal.

Yet the paradox remains that a person is born bourgeois. And for a long time now historians and sociologists have held that

the chief difficulty about becoming bourgeois is that it is not something one does on one's own. Everybody belongs to a family before he belongs to a class. It is through his [or of course her] family that the person who is bourgeois-born is bourgeois, because it is with the family that he becomes such. (Goblot 1980)

It takes three generations, we were told, to make a bourgeois, and in this respect all our informants belong to a fully mature bourgeoisie. A study of their family and genealogical memory (the subject of this final chapter) does in fact lie at the origin of the work presented here. The work itself has a history. Several years previously, while investigating this same subject of family memory, though in a part of Paris's thirteenth district where at that time various social strata were living side by side, I was led to an overwhelmingly simple conclusion: certain people were well endowed with relations and memories while others appeared to have been cheated of them. Could Bourdieu's seemingly caricatural suggestion be true, namely that relations are attracted to relations as capital is attracted to capital?[1]

Before exploring the family memory of the bourgeois, I had to answer the following questions: what kind of memory am I looking for? Once again, I needed to consider the survey situation and take into account the 'complex

---

[1] 'One only has to ask oneself why and how the powerful have all those nephews, great-nephews, and great-great-nephews to realise that, if the most important people also have the largest families whereas 'poor relations' are also the poorest in relations, it is because, in this field as elsewhere, capital flows to capital' (Bourdieu 1972).

web of relationships that forms between observers and observed' (Zonabend 1986).

The investigator gathers a discourse that he/she is responsible for stimulating and provoking. For a certain number of hours over several days the informant will put together and deliver an account of his/her family history. It is an unusual exercise, and it can be a disturbing one. As an act of speech, memory thus elicited will need to be placed in the context of the respective social statuses of the interlocutors. Indeed, memory data gathered in this way provide an archaeology of the first stratum of family memory as much as a representation of the relations that exist between an individual and the society in which he or she lives. And the frontier between strictly family memories and those evoking the social settings to which those memories belong becomes blurred if not actually artificial. This is why my study of family memory led me on to this study of milieu, the social environment in which such memory takes shape and is handed down. The memory to which the ethnologist gains access is thus cloaked in social significance. As for affective memory (the latent content of memory), it will remain essentially mysterious. The fieldwork situation leaves no room for confusion: the kind of recollection produced by work of a psychoanalytical nature has nothing to do with that evoked by the presence of the investigator. And even if this encouragement to 'talk family' produces a series of ill-controlled emotional reactions it will always leave the question of 'the subject' outside its purview.

Our aim being to bring out the specific character of bourgeois memory, it would seem to be necessary to compare it with that of other kinds. To effect such a comparison, we propose to draw on the findings of certain studies carried out in French peasant circles (Segalen 1985 and Zonabend 1980) and among middle-class Parisians (Le Wita 1984). However, before any comparison can be made, it is essential that we set out certain problems of method.

If, as Bergson believed, memory is a function of intelligence, and if we take intelligence to mean the sum of an individual's cultural acquisitions, the time limit on the interviews and the means employed may have magnified if not created inequalities. For example, in the investigation carried out in the thirteenth district, the suggestion that people might like to trace their genealogies had elicited a certain number of reactions that all revealed the social imprint of the request. Very quickly a contrast had became apparent between popular strata and middle or upper strata. The former, undoubtedly complying with the principle of strict necessity (getting straight to the point, only saying what really matters), did not readily mention their deceased grandparents, whereas the latter, with an intuitive knowledge of ethnology, sought to evoke not only their great-grandparents but ancestors even more remote.

So to restrict questioning about memory to genealogy would have deepened the silence of some and enhanced the volubility of others. By varying the tools of inquiry, it was possible to bring some compensation into play. For instance, semi-directed interviews showed that family memory among non-peasant working-class people does not necessarily run on genealogical lines but comes out more readily as an account of something experienced. So genealogical data have to be distinguished from family memory. Conversely, questions can be asked about the extent to which bourgeois memory is affected by the written word, for surely what the ethnologist is collecting is the spoken written word, a lesson more or less well learned? Memorising genealogical data requires an obvious effort. Indeed, there is no more thankless task than remembering strings of names and dates and quasi-official information about dead or unknown relations. Moreover, knowing how to place oneself in and move through genealogical space presupposes a certain training. It became clear during interviews that the informant was constantly having to find landmarks in order not to get lost in the immaterial world represented by a kindred expressed in genealogical terms. Memorisation of such data may thus be wholly dependent on socio-cultural variables. Its educational and cultural capital would place the bourgeoisie at an advantage here. Indeed, the bourgeois educational system regards the development of memory as fundamental to that of intelligence, and what might be described as a collective training of this faculty takes place within bourgeois families. It was not unusual during interviews to hear poems recited, for example, or bits of plays reproduced; a stock of quotations learned by heart circulated like so many passwords among members of the group. So a whole complex of cultural factors would give bourgeois informants an advantage, which might account for their ability to recall their more remote ancestry in greater detail than other interviewees. In fact, though, family records, albums and written genealogies play only a secondary role in the learning of family history. Proofs in writing of membership of the bourgeoisie merely set the seal on a status already acquired and acknowledged by others. Those concerned express a polite lack of interest, a detachment that has nothing negative about it: 'it is the privilege of privileges, the one that consists in taking liberties with one's privilege' (Bourdieu 1982). In the bourgeoisie, memory operates like capital that is accumulated and handed down through several generations. Within families, genealogy circulates innately. One does not search for one's roots; they are there, forming part of one. Learning genealogical data off by heart would make no sense in the circumstances. Moreover, the exercise would be quite separate from the normal processes of communication.

So let us try, in the light of all this, to compare family and genealogical memory in the bourgeoisie with family and genealogical memory among the working and lower-middle classes in town and country.

The first thing such a comparison brings out is the diversity of types of memory. If people do not remember in all societies, it is also true that within a

24  The privilege of privileges
Written proof (the family tree) merely confirms a status already acquired and already acknowledged by others. That is why people politely indicate a lack of interest. It is a detachment that has
nothing negative about it: 'It is simply the privilege of privileges, the one that consists in taking
liberties with one's privilege' (Bourdieu 1982).

single society people do not remember in the same way. The diversity is in
terms of two factors: the scope and precision of a genealogical viewpoint, and
the narrative method used to recount family history. The common ground
has to do with the processes of memorisation.

## An extensive, detailed memory

In the study done in Paris's thirteenth district, of 148 persons interviewed
more than half had mentioned between 26 and 100 relations; 8 had
mentioned over 100. Half the bourgeois informants mentioned between 50
and 100 relatives, the other half between 150 and 300. The size of the
number of relations recalled is clearly dependent on demographic data. Let
us, for example, take the memory of Mr Pierre I. (aged 60). This informant
belongs to an old family of Paris solicitors. Their genealogy may be found in a
compendium (Delavenne, *Le Recueil généalogique de la bourgeoisie ancienne*)
published in 1954. Mr Pierre I. senior also has his own genealogy, listing all
his collaterals and their many descendants. This group is so extensive that Mr
Pierre I. was obliged, at the time of his marriage, to revise the 'family card

25  The shrine of memory I

'In one corner of the drawing-room there is my little photo collection, everyone goes and has a
look at that. The desk belonged to my paternal grandmother. It holds photos of our children,
brothers and sisters-in-law, my mother's five grandchildren: they are my very, very dearest ones'
(Mrs O. junior).

index' belonging to his father. 'My wife was marrying into an enormous family', he explained, 'and needed to become acquainted with it.' It is impossible to do full justice to his memory here; suffice it to say that, without consulting the card index and claiming to be 'not very good at this', Mr Pierre I. recalled more than 150 relations. With the help of the card index he was able to present a family with more than 300 members. Demographic factors largely account for the size of that family.

Mr Pierre I. has three sons and one daughter. His three sons, none of them over thirty-five, already have three children each; his daughter, who is younger, has two. The informant's sister had eight children, six of whom have between three and five children of their own. Mr Pierre I. has thirty-five cousins on his mother's side. Most of them have between five and nine children. His father had only one half-brother, but that half-brother had seven children, one of whom has twelve children, two others six and so on. Looking at the descendants of the three brothers of Ego's maternal grandfather, we find that the first had five children, two of whom were childless and the other three had four children each, two of whom in turn had six children of their own and the others three each. Mr Pierre I. sees this group (comprising some thirty persons) regularly. The second brother produced eight children, all of whom are married and have children themselves. Ego also frequents that branch of the family. As for the third brother, he fathered nine children:

Of those, two are nuns, one died in the war without issue, and another married but had no offspring. Two of them had five children, all married with at least three children of their own. There is one who had six children, but I don't know them. I can easily find them in the card index.

It is traditional in certain families 'to produce six or seven children', a tradition that provides the members of those families with vast kindreds. The families where more than 100 relations were mentioned are examples; the others recorded a lower birth-rate (one or two children per generation). The number of relations mentioned gives no indication as to the range and accuracy of memory.

All the bourgeois informants mentioned the members making up the phratries of their four grandparents. In the thirteenth district, no interviewee had mentioned such relations. Only sixteen had been able to recall the brothers and sisters of both maternal grandparents. However, if we move to a rural environment – to Minot in Burgundy, for example, where Albertine displays 'an immense lateral genealogical memory' (Zonabend 1980), or South Bigouden in Brittany, where 'knowledge of collaterality proves to be detailed in the extreme' (Segalen 1985) – it seems there is nothing particularly special about bourgeois memory in this regard.

On the other hand, when it comes to genealogical depth members of the bourgeoisie do stand out (together with descendants of the nobility) from

26  The shrine of memory II

Mrs O. senior's photo corner in the bathroom, comprising a portrait painting of her mother, wedding photos of her eldest daughter, photos of her children and other close relations (brothers and sisters with their spouses, nephews and nieces), and a picture of her house, painted by herself. There is also a photograph of Marshal Lyautey, who was her godfather.

other social groups. Here once again is Mr Pierre I. senior (who can easily recall three generations of antecedents, enabling him to cover six generations in all):

I had five great-uncles on my mother's side. They had their father and two uncles. Those three brothers were descended from one Saturnin X, who was married to a B. I was always hearing people talk about that B. family. I know there are books, but in my present state I can't tell you anything precise.

Mr Pierre I. is no isolated instance. Indeed, bourgeois memories very often go back beyond the great-grandparents. In the thirteenth district, 8 people (all of executive rank) had done the same. But only 19 out of 148 had mentioned their great-grandparents. They had gone into genealogy for the repeated clues that it contained foreshadowing their own current position in society. M.L., for example, a bookseller aged 55, told us how his paternal great-grandfather had been a publisher in Paris. A similar case was Mrs F., a 28-year-old teacher who recalled that her maternal great-grandmother had been 'awarded the Legion of Honour as the best schoolteacher in Haute-Savoie department'. The authors of a recent study of the occupational roots of workers and senior managers in France also point out that only individuals belonging to the upper classes (and this has been so for a long time, they note) 'best remember the occupational histories of their grand-parents' (Thélot and de Singly 1986). Rootedness in a particular social stratum certainly seems to be a decisive factor as regards memorisation of genealogical data. In Minot, on the other hand, Françoise Zonabend notes that memory in depth is 'rare' two or three generations above the interviewee (Zonabend 1980). In South Bigouden [Brittany],

genealogical memories do not go back very far. Often one grandparental patronymic in four has been forgotten, and in the case of great-grandparents the proportion is even higher. The genealogies reconstituted here [in her book] orally, in interviews, are shallow in depth and soon peter out. (Segalen 1985)

In all these memories, however different from one social group to another, grandparents represent a key element, operating for some people as a sort of 'stop'. For the population at large, not including the affluent classes, grandparents do indeed appear to constitute the limit of people's genealogical memory. In our society, as in others, the varying capacities of individuals to recall genealogical data depend on the social use they make of such data, not on their intrinsic intellectual skills. As Jack Goody says, it is all closely bound up with 'a pre-existent social order' (Goody 1977).

## Social uses of kinship

Apart from the close family (frequently very numerous) with whom the bourgeois interviewees had regular contact, the kindred as a whole formed

27 La Guette is 100 years old!

It happened in 1881 ...
Marie G., widow of Eugène L., completed construction of the house known as La Guette.
It was particularly intended for young Charles, then aged 18, whose delicate health
appeared to require that he live in the country.
That was a hundred years ago ...
To celebrate this centenary, Marie-Madeleine and Roger will be delighted to receive you
at La Guette on Sunday 5 July.
Mass said at the house around 12 o'clock by Pierre and Robert will be followed by a
frugal country repast.
They count on you coming and thank you for your affirmative reply, which they hope to
receive by 20 June.

the object of a veritable social practice: one's uncle was one's solicitor, one's
solicitor was one's uncle. Mr Pierre I. senior lives in an apartment building
that has been in his mother's family for three generations. Numerous
descendants still live there, so they meet on a daily basis. Of his more distant
relations, he often sees a doctor (who has become the family's doctor), a
surgeon (who has become the family's surgeon), an inspector of taxes (who
has become the family's financial adviser), and a top architect in the
Department of Historical Monuments (currently advising the family in
connection with some building work that needs to be done on the family
château). The way in which people will often use patronymics is indicative of
this social relationship to the kindred. This is the reason, for example, why
Mrs Laure C. senior (grandmother) declined during our interview to list all
the members of her kindred. 'It's an impossible task', she said. And an

unnecessary one, she might have added. In fact, she has no need to memorise their names and addresses, saying that she uses the *Bottin mondain*. She is able, starting from a limited number of patronymics and tracing marriages, to find the name of this or that more remote relation. Uncle Louis's family are called Duteil, Aunt Yolande's family are called Verdon, the Duteils happen to be married to the Duponts, who are close friends of the Verdons, and so on. These family and social worlds appear almost impenetrably complex. In fact, bourgeois families will put themselves forward as micro-societies, where one seeks to be self-sufficient [*à vivre entre soi*]. Geneviève described how her mother would find it inconceivable, for example, that she should purchase her sheets herself in the Descamps discount store beneath where she lives: 'one has to go, on the pretext that he is family, through cousin Descamps, whom I never see'. People will go to enormous lengths to find reasons for using relations or friends of relations.

On the pretext of economy, people will set in motion the most amazingly cumbersome systems. Be it wine, foie gras, medicine, whatever – there is no question of buying it anywhere but in the family. (Geneviève)

The pretext of economy is an explicit shift, turning the family network into a private social network. It is a question of bringing everyone into one's own little world. An anecdote is relevant here. A friend told Geneviève's mother that her son was about to marry the daughter of a professor of medicine. The professor in question happened to be Geneviève's mother's doctor. Hearing the news, she exclaimed: 'She's a really charming girl.' It was a white lie (she did not know the girl). By saying what she did Geneviève's mother was signifying to her friend that she was not a total stranger to this family that would so soon be enlarging their circle. Also, relations between Geneviève's mother and her doctor (the professor of medicine) would be strengthened by this fresh tie.

We find ourselves immersed in the atmosphere of Proust's *A la recherche du temps perdu*, where people take such delight in disentangling genealogical threads and deciphering the nature of the relationships that exist between individuals and families. Identifying what is special about bourgeois family memory inevitably leads us to take account of the place this social group occupies in society. In the process, we rediscover at the oral level the same phenomenon as historians encounter at the level of written sources, namely that the abundance of some is matched by the paucity of others. Very clearly, in fact, this genealogical knowledge is not of equal interest to all social groups. This seems to be proven by the reactions of South Bigouden countryfolk when the investigator, having reconstituted numerous genealogies, shows them to the parties concerned:

They are not interested in knowing their ascendant kin. This is because they have no need to establish an identity or find roots; they have always known that they belonged

28 Family seats II

In these vast damp dwellings the members of the clan breathe in an atmosphere of antiquity.

to and were a part of this region, and having the fact confirmed strikes them as merely futile. On the other hand those who had left the district or whose job put a distance between themselves and the village placed a high value on their family tree as furnishing proof of identity and local roots. (Segalen 1985)

The family memory of countryfolk and the family memory of the bourgeois have in common the fact of being closely bound up with social practices. However, for countryfolk there is no necessity for retaining names since everyone in the village community knows what needs to be known. Bourgeois memory, on the other hand (equally intimately known and equally diffused within the family circle), needs to be precise, offering a detailed collection of names and dates. The one kind has a range confined to the village community while the other occupies a national if not an international stage and frequently has a public dimension. Indeed, the memory of a bourgeois family may supply a chapter in the economic, financial or political history of France.

## The props of memory

However, if bourgeois informants are capable of citing their grandparents and even more distant ascendants, they do not commit all the lines of their genealogies to memory, and for them too the grandparents constitute a 'stop', a symbolic, emotional cut-off point associated with the very process of transmission and the peculiar dynamics of recall. This is precisely where the researcher perceives the influence of the written word on the discourse being gathered. Beyond the grandparents, informants will insert qualifiers to express the fact that they did not witness what they are 'recounting' at first hand (for example, 'I was always told that . . .', 'Grandmother used to say that . . .', and so on). Here too the grandparents become the limit of personal recollection, the limit (in effect) of direct transmission of the sort that each individual controls and manipulates as he or she wishes. Where the first-hand witnesses are still alive, subsequent generations pass on the family history only 'diffidently'. Its transmission, closely bound up with the family's life cycle, is governed by a kind of birthright. The three women of the Laure C. family (grandmother, daughter, granddaughter) are well aware of this. The Laure C. family has for two centuries belonged to the solid industrial bourgeoisie; it has its own records and numerous volumes recounting its history. The grandmother, aged 88, is capable of citing distant ascendants, but fearing she will not be understood by her descendants she makes her mother the strong figure on the paternal side; her own daughter, aged 55, hands down the same information. As for the granddaughter, aged 32, she invests her living grandmother with the same symbolic attributes as the grandmother acknowledges her own mother to have possessed. It is only the second generation that echoes the discourse of the previous generation

29 Heirlooms I

'On the table in the hall stand two Chinese vases that belonged to my maternal grandmother. In the middle is an old box bearing the coat-of-arms of my husband's family, surrounding by photographs and by some paintings on wood that were done by a paternal great-aunt around 1900' (Mrs O. junior).

unchanged. The third generation relies on the living ancestor as first-hand witness of the most remote traces of the family history. In the process of transmission, three generations form a minimum to generate a condition of stability and represent a maximum as regards allowing individual appropriation. It thus takes three generations for assimilation to the bourgeois condition to take place, for individual and collective interests to achieve a balance and for a person to fit naturally into his or her cultural world. A link needs to be established with Legendre's analyses concerning the genealogical principle in the West.

A generation does not exist in isolation; it is not an age class or a school year but a synthesis of at least two generations or, as Virgil suggests, three generations. The whole *Aeneid* is based on the tacit assumption that the son is involved with his father and with his father's father. (Legendre 1985)

Genealogy consists in making room, in making the 'subject' pass from the biological to the cultural order; it consists in 'causing the subject to be reborn in the order of institutions' (*ibid*.). There is a thread to be traced here, drawing a parallel between genealogy as a rational demand and bourgeois education as the learning of a code of behaviour.

Bourgeois memory may go beyond the grandparents to trace the ascendant lines of genealogy, recalling what are sometimes extremely remote origins. As

30 Living memory

Mr O. senior's bedroom contains a fine example of living memory, constantly being updated.

3·1 Heirlooms II

'The cockerels were wedding presents, the pear-shaped vases belonged to my mother-in-law' (Mrs O. senior).

in a narrow defile, light penetrates the gorges of genealogy as far as the third stage, after which there is a more or less grey area, with the light at the end of the tunnel being provided by the real or imagined origins of the family. The date when a particular patronymic appeared is an easy symbol to memorise.

Bourgeois memory is twofold: in emotional and family terms it can be likened to any other kind of family memory; in genealogical and social terms it is unique, being charged with handing down a particular status and a feeling of belonging to a group. A person is bourgeois by family, not by blood or by divine right. Each generation has therefore, by the light of the one before it, to maintain the status acquired. Genealogical memory thus serves to guard against the inherent frailty of the bourgeois position yet can only be handed down by incorporating family memory. And the processes of recall present these two memories in a special combination.

## The processes of memorisation

### A way of talking family

Like every story, the (hi)story[2] of the family is one that is told. Certain members of the kindred thus find themselves credited with a detailed knowledge of the family's past as well as with particular skill at remembering. Very often it is the grandparents. Listening to the accounts of these people endowed with the gift of memory and a greater ability than others to keep that memory circulating among the generations, I was struck by how small a role was played in them by nostalgia. This was in contrast to what I had found earlier in the thirteenth district, where the recollection of memories invariably generated lively regrets about the past, turning it into a veritable golden age. In fact, according to Halbwachs this is a structural feature: 'The great majority of people are aware at moments of greater or lesser frequency of what might be called a nostalgia for the past' (Halbwachs 1975). Halbwachs makes this relationship to the past a law of humanity, saying that constraint is not felt except when in operation, and a past constraint is by definition no longer in operation. Society thus functions on the forgetting of constraints. For 'if man saw only the constraint of the past, he would have no impulse towards society' (*ibid.*). To say of bourgeois memory that it is characterised by an absence of nostalgia could be misunderstood. I am not trying to say that the bourgeois are free of this irresistible attraction exercised by the past; I merely wish to emphasise strongly that they do not make the feeling of nostalgia the basic fabric of their account. What we get is a discourse in which nostalgia is contained, held in check, kept in the speaker's possession.

---

[2]  English, in retaining both the full and aphetic forms of the word, has invented a distinction of which French is innocent [Tr.].

32 Mr O.'s study

'He used to disappear there every Saturday afternoon. Mr O. was particularly fond of this 1925 desk, which had belonged to his father. On it he kept photographs of his father, his children, and the family estate' (Mrs O. junior).

33 The guest room

A guest room contains a portrait of Mrs O. senior's grandmother.

34 The china collection

'In the dining-room there is a splendid ancestral bust surrounded by a whole collection of blue and white porcelain' (Mrs O. junior).

For example, bourgeois who experienced glorious times in the past (masses of servants, holidays, lavish parties) may occasionally have seen their way of life become less luxurious and their standard of living decline, but this does not give rise to any talk of calamity. This is how it goes, they will say; every life has its hard times and its happy days, the one succeeding the other. In the light of those that have gone before, each generation has a certain duty to perform, faced with the fresh reality that it encounters. The account will seek above all to pass on this kind of moral imposition. So the containment of nostalgia is more the result of an effort of self-discipline intended to establish communication between generations than a frame of mind personally characterising the speaker.

Again, though, it is very hard to dissociate acquired factors from those that are inherited, because the need to establish communication between the generations is closely bound up with the renewal/reconstruction of the bourgeois condition. So handing down the code largely determines the way in which family history is told. Informants sought to limit any kind of expression of emotion. For example, they very rarely indulged in personal judgements. If one did slip out, they would apologise and be careful to add that they were voicing nothing but commonplaces shared by other members of the family. 'There's no denying it – grandmother was alarmingly authoritative', or 'grandfather well and truly did for the family fortune, but in those days that happened frequently', or possibly 'Uncle Charles was a twit, a stupid, narrow-minded fool'.

This manner of speaking is basically no more than a literal translation of bourgeois cultural schemata. It is mainly a question of avoiding familiarity and keeping a distance between oneself and one's family history. The speaker is not forever inserting himself or herself into the account that he or she is giving and is responsible for handing down. Any kind of expressive content is kept under control. The bourgeois way of recounting family history may be likened to the rules of politeness in that both are based on 'an infinitely nuanced skill at marking distances'. As a result, the account takes on a certain objectivity that enhances its credibility.

For example, few personal memories are recalled, by which is meant memories that place the feelings of the subject at the centre of the events or anecdotes recounted. This distance observed in relation to the speaker's own history to some extent reflects the family usages and practices within which he/she grew up.

As a child, the speaker was always surrounded by brothers and sisters, cousins, nurses and governesses. It was a tribal existence, limiting the frequency of dual relationships; only exceptionally did the child find itself alone with its father or mother. All informants of both sexes expressed the feeling of having 'belonged to vast networks'. Formerly, large domestic staffs and extensive grounds made it materially easier to learn self-control and the practice of distance in the sense of standing back from oneself, so to speak, or of the speaker standing back from what he/she is saying. Nowadays families are increasingly becoming 'nuclear' and children are very often brought up by their parents directly (rather than through nannies, for example). Learning the art of distance is no longer as easy as it once was.

This accounts for the anxiety of the younger generation with regard to what is to become of the family seats (places where the distinguishing marks are acquired naturally) and its almost obsessive attachment to the rules of politeness and to table manners. This focusing on usages involves their being spelled out; it means adults are having to explain to their children in formal terms what is in fact inexplicable. However, coercing oneself into these codes of behaviour means being able to form part of the family; it means taking one's place in the family's history. That history must not be allowed to become a 'dead letter'; it must be heard and memorised and then recalled and handed down.

## A history run through with red threads and dotted with red patches

Herodotus's history has been described as fragmentary, made up of isolated events and frozen tableaux. Time hurries on when something happens, stops when something is being described, even goes backwards if having spoken of the son it becomes necessary to look at the father. In a nutshell, Herodotus's history does not unfold; the successive actions of men do not form a 'red thread' but 'red patches' (Focke, quoted in Meyerson 1956). The metaphor captures two conceptions of time: one linear, the other cyclical. It contrasts chronology with genealogy.

Recounting family history syncretises these two conceptions. Informants situate their memories in a period of time; they associate dates with particular events, recall moments of national history. The narrative stretches itself out or telescopes, depending on whether it is ascending or descending the line of chronology. But it may equally favour a cyclical view of time, dwelling on a particular individual, highlighting a particular genealogical moment, amplifying a particular sequence. Family memory constitutes an indissoluble blend of uniqueness and order.

Paradoxically, the red threads that the speaker draws are to the narrative what the concern with genealogy is to memory: they serve to pass on the feeling of belonging to the group. Certain themes stand out. Cultural atmosphere (from education to leisure activities), work (invariably presented as a distinctive moral value), and marriages (which literally produce the heirs) provide veritable narrative seams that informants will mine to the point of exhaustion. Take Mr Georges H. senior, for instance. At the conclusion of our interviews he summed up what constitutes the essence of his memory:

35 The salient bits of memory
'Aunt Yolande: the nose is famous in the family' (Mrs O. senior).

What chiefly interests me in the history of the family is the childhood of my mother and of my uncles and aunts. One sees unfolding there a scene of bourgeois simplicity set in spacious apartments entirely given over to hospitality. One finds the same simplicity in terms of leisure activities, from the theatre [specifically, the *Opéra comique*] to renting villas for the summer. Relations with the aristocracy were unstrained. There are memories associated with politics, a grandfather who was violently anti-Dreyfus, memories associated with marriages and go-betweens, practical jokes, and finally a strict and omnipresent religion. (Mr Georges H. senior)

These narrative motifs were sketched in against a background in which time ran very swiftly. Speakers recalled 'the day we used to go to Granny's', English nannies, the cook, outings in the Bois de Boulogne, the first cars and the family chauffeur, arranged marriages and the amount of dowry paid – memories that belonged to a bygone age ('almost antediluvian', as Mrs Emilie E. remarked). They also spoke of concerns relating to the present: women going to work, common-law marriages, divorce, religious and moral values. Wars, political disputes and the economic development of the country also found their way into such accounts. All these memories thus recalled a life-style and a way of being, thinking and acting peculiar to the group. But they would not get through, they would not be heard, if they were not accompanied by 'red patches'. These are the elements of memory that the individual captures personally and chooses to call his or her own. The memorising of family history necessarily proceeds by way of individual re-appropriation, because 'in reality everyone uses his genealogy as he wishes and manipulates his identity' (Zonabend 1986).

Choices are made. Every ethnologist who has studied the family has found that, in our society, where filiation is undifferentiated, family memory and family contact are selective. 'This selectivity both in genealogy and in choice of relationship is in fact one of the distinguishing features of the European kinship system' (Segalen 1981).

Broadly speaking, the genealogical memory of the bourgeois seems fairly unselective. The patronymic may be a fundamental notion (occasionally reinforced by the handing down of forenames), but that does not mean the maternal relations are any the less familiar. However, genealogical memory is not the whole of family memory. Selectivity comes in at the level of what has been termed 'affective' or 'elective memory'. This type of memory can be seen in the choice and abundance of things recalled. We note that such recollections tend to relate more to the maternal side of the family and to female elements in the kindred. So selectivity exists, but it does not operate at the level of strict awareness; it operates at the emotional level and is the product of transmission. Thus Mr Louis G. senior (grandfather), wholly wrapped up in the succession of 'the males' of his family, did not forget that it was through his mother that he had inherited. He dwelt at length on the 'adoration' he felt for this woman. All his 'delightful' and 'enchanting' memories stemmed from her, he said.

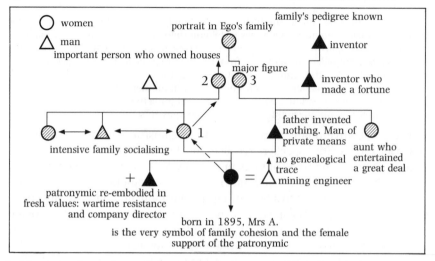

1. 'Mummy used to see her mother every day. Mummy was a *demoiselle* F. She was very pretty and very musical. She played the piano very well. We used to play four-handed classical music with her here (in the house) every evening.'
2. 'My grandmother had been widowed very young and lived very handsomely on the profits of the distillery. She very soon owned a motor car, a superb Panhard, with chauffeur, very shortly after motor cars came in.'
3. 'My grandmother was a delightful woman, charming, very pretty, very elegant, very much a woman of the world, she gave marvellous parties and was extremely musical.'

Genealogical diagram 1

Mrs Arnold A. professed enormous admiration for the men of her family, feeling herself to be the heiress of the founders of the dynasty. But in connection with these 'heroes' it was of their wives and mothers that she talked at length (see genealogical diagram 1).

Take the example of the Georges H. family again. Messrs Georges H. senior and junior have memory fields closely bound up with their maternal relations. Consequently, the family identifications of father and son are quite different. The father sees his identity as stemming from his mother's family. In that family he finds the 'glorious' male ancestor to be his maternal grandfather. He is attached to his patronymic but gives meaning to it only because of its association with his mother's name.

As for the son, he states:

I place myself more in relation to the T.s [his mother's maternal family]. I have no identification with the L.s [his father's maternal family]. We used to go to the Tuileries [gardens] with the L.s. There were also the lease renewals on 1 January. That went on for as long as the tenancies. Why the T.s? The other family was certainly the prestigious one. And then there's Les Essarts, as my mother's family's château is called. The summers of my boyhood. That's the main reason. (Mr Georges H., junior; see genealogical diagram 2)

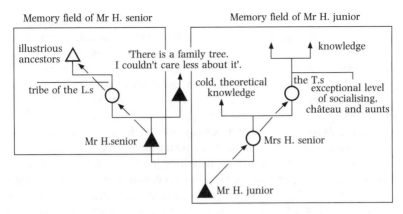

Genealogical diagram 2

Finally let us turn to the example of the Laure C. family. Here we have a case of extreme simplification, grandmother, mother and daughter all having made the same choice in that they see their ties as being with the maternal family. The daughter upheld the choice vehemently:

The maternal branch constitutes my family a hundred thousand times more than my father's branch. It's an initiation into things, a cultural environment, the things I love, a very strong feeling of belonging to a large family. (Laure C. junior)

If these women inspired so many delightful and enchanting memories it is because, as we have seen, they were at the heart of the transmission of bourgeois culture.

As the young wife of Mr Pierre I. junior remarked:

We all have the same background. We were brought up by women. Some people attach more importance than others to this or that. In the education of children, there are some things that take first place. For instance, it infuriates me when I see my nephews nibble at fruit and leave it virtually untouched. (Mrs Pierre I. junior)

The remarks are typical of one who has 'married in', a *pièce rapportée* (see footnote 4, p. 47).

Beyond these trivia (though we know how important they can be), women humanise genealogical memory (the kind that merely retains the succession of the male representatives of a family). They establish a link between the social and private worlds, between the individual and the tribe; it is through them that the fusion between social identity and family identity takes place.

The vehemence of the remarks of Laure C. junior ushers us into the holy of holies of memory, namely the place where individual re-appropriation occurs. There is something deeply moving about listening to these stories, which are all alike yet are all experienced as unique. In the course of oral transmission, memories of family events and personalities jostle one another, and we witness what is really a process of erosion in which each person frees the salient parts with which he/she will identify and that will make him/her want to believe in them. From this standpoint, each family history is individual and unique. An uncle out in the East driving an eggshell-blue Chrysler, a great-grandmother who rode side-saddle, a great-uncle who owns a Capuchin monastery, a distant ancestress who was mistress to Louis XV ... Hearing such family legends gives one a feeling of extreme diversity in which the dominant feature is the distinctive nature of each individual destiny. People speak of a particular physical, moral or other peculiarity supposedly inherent in the group. With the I.s it is the way they laugh and their hospitality, with the C.s their attachment to the steel industry, with the A.s their courage and beauty, with the B.s their love of mountaineering, with the E.s the fact that the men die of heart attacks, and so on. There is infinite variety in the qualities that may come to symbolise a group, providing the armorial bearings of memory, so to speak. Like the games people play on the fringes of table manners or forms of politeness, these symbolic details help to establish 'family idiosyncracies'.

So there is no true (hi)story of the family. Every memory, by its very nature, is a translation. There is no point, in the circumstances, in searching for the original model; it is better to confine our attention to the anecdotes, the little things that provoke big reactions:

To me, belonging to the bourgeoisie is a blend of traditions and values in the broad sense, solidarities, the stories one tells. When I was a lad my great-uncle, an Egyptologist, took me to the Place de la Concorde and read me what it said on the obelisk. That was P.-L., a nicer man than his brother. He could read the hieroglyphics: they were part of my culture. The obelisk belonged to me much more than to the fellahs.

Red patches or hard kernels of memory all spring from the symbolic labour performed by each individul when he/she memorises and passes on the family's history. 'This symbolic arrangement eventually creates its own paths in memory, those evocations that the slightest thing will trigger and that nothing, it seems, can stop' (Sperber 1974).

# CONCLUSION

This study sprang from a personal irritation. Why, I wanted to know, are there these people whom society (without actually saying so) calls 'bourgeois'? Why may we not put a name to something that stares each one of us in the face at some time or another? In other words, why the inverted commas?

One approach (a classic one in the human sciences) consisted in starting from the word. Here we can echo what Braudel says of capital: drive it out of the door, and it will come straight back in through the window (Braudel 1979). For eight centuries there has teemed, behind all the rhetoric of defamation and denial, a varied and complex world made up of men and women whose destinies are written over the space of more than three generations. Yet neither their social attributes nor their innate quality allow us to call them bourgeois. That meant studying their culture.

To help us we had a body of informants who will certainly not have said all that they have to say once and for all. Pressed with questions, obliged to locate themselves, and led to admit to being bourgeois, they supplied verbal testimony. At the same time, they also revealed themselves in visual terms. The elusive aspect of their behaviour was, to some small extent, captured and inevitably reduced.

How, then, could one help but be aware of the extraordinary aberration that consisted in thus taking lens and microscope to the study of the customs of a group about which thousands upon thousands of pages have been written in the past, a group that has dominated and deeply influenced society as a whole?

These trivia, detected and undoubtedly magnified by the method, have a particular function, namely to create distinction. They are experienced by our bourgeois individuals as specifically human traits. This takes us back to Erasmus's conception of man, according to which man finds in his quality as man something that is self-evidently, naturally his, something to which he clings in order to govern his existence. It is what enables him to mark out a sphere for himself in which he will live with himself and his fellows. If something unfamiliar should then take him by surprise or elude his grasp, he is at least master of himself: he knows himself. His close fellows will reflect a

36  Le Gué Gaillard, drawn by Mariel
'A lovely house indeed, but not in the family any more . . .' (drawing lent by Mrs F.).

precise image of the way one should be; the ritualisation of his daily life will shield him against the silly mistakes he so much dreads making. The whole person of the bourgeois, from appearance to voice modulations, is thus imbued with the values and cultural schemata of the group. And the thing by which these men and women set such store is experienced by them as belonging to humankind as such, to all 'civilised' beings. Erasmus's project of drawing up a code of conduct common to all men, based on the reduction of idiosyncracies, was a failure in that specific characteristics persisted. Possibly that of the bourgeois is to consign the subject and his/her psychological adventures to the background. It is a remarkable characteristic in a society that has seen the emergence of a steadily more sustained attention to (not to say hypertrophy of) the self.

Jealous guardians of a middle position, the bourgeois paradoxically insist on being seized in motion. So perhaps it is impossible to put a name to them. Their life is sufficient proof that they place themselves right at the centre of life. In which case, who can possibly decipher something that so completely goes without saying?

## APPENDIX

Brief biographies of forty-nine young women educated at Sainte Marie colleges, including their views on the principal qualities and defects of their education.

*Béatrice*, b. 1956, started at Sainte Marie college as an infant because 'it was nearby and recommended'.

Two sisters at Sainte Marie, a brother at Franklin [the Jesuit boys' school Saint Louis de Gonzague, popularly known as 'Franklin' from the name of the Paris street in which it is situated].

Quality: 'academic standard'.

Defect: 'not very open to the outside world. Thinks it is the centre of the universe. Non-coeducational. Uselessness of Catholic education. To me, Sainte Marie moulds fairly individualistic, not always realistic intellectuals. Poor preparation for higher education.'

Takes the old girls' magazine [*Bulletin de l'association des Anciennes*].

Went on to study history and librarianship and worked as a librarian 1976–82. Currently taking a diploma in graphology.

Father's occupation: high-ranking civil servant at the National Assembly. Mother's occupation: none.

Béatrice got married in church in 1979. Husband a personnel manager. They have two children.

*Catherine*, b. 1955, started at Sainte Marie in 1959: 'Mother is a Sainte Marie old girl and thinks the world of it.'

Aunts and a sister of Catherine's went to Sainte Marie; a brother went to Saint Louis de Gonzague.

For reasons of geographical distance, her daughters attend a state (nursery) school.

Quality: 'open-mindedness and curiosity'.

Defect: 'pupils not given enough independence'.

Went on to study law and obtained a master's degree. Worked as a management assistant 1980–2 and as a trainee accountant 1982–6.

Father's occupation: management assistant. Mother's occupation: company manager.

Catherine got married in church in 1980. Husband a highly qualified telecommunications engineer.

*Pascale*, b. 1955, does not know why her parents sent her to Sainte Marie: 'Not having seen my parents since receiving your document, I am afraid I cannot answer your question, never having asked them in fact.'

A sister went to Sainte Marie, a brother to Saint Jean de Passy.

On the subject of her children, who are all at Catholic private schools: 'There is no Sainte Marie in Reims. I always said that if I stayed in Paris I would not send my daughters to Sainte Marie, wanting a change, but my son goes to Saint Joseph de Reims, which has many points in common with what I used to know!!'

Quality: 'a spirit of organisation and synthesis, very useful in everyday life. A method of working.'

Defect: '1) possibly excessive cramming, a method I am finding again at Saint Joseph. At the time I saw it as such, yet today I can see the difference between what my son knows and what other children know (while still moaning occasionally about all the work they give him!!); 2) rather too academic an education, poor preparation for the material aspects of house-keeping (e.g. sewing, etc.).'

Not a member of the old girls' association.

Went on to study history. Started but did not complete a master's degree. Has never worked.

Father's occupation: wine grower.

Pascale got married in church in 1977 and has four children. Her husband is a qualified wine grower.

*Bénédicte*, b. 1956, started at Sainte Marie in 1962 for 'moral and religious' reasons.

Aunts and cousins also went there.

Brothers and sisters: Sainte Marie, Janson de Sailly [a *lycée* frequented by the bourgeois], Sainte Croix de Neuilly.

If she had daughters of school age she would not send them to Sainte Marie.

Quality: 'reliability'.

Defect: 'direction'.

Not a member of the old girls' association.

Went on to study classics and obtain a master's degree. Has had various jobs since 1978, including teaching.

Father's occupation: engineer. Mother's occupation: secretary.

Bénédicte is living in a common-law marriage. Her partner, a qualified engineer, does 'reliability research' for Electricité de France.

*Honorine*, b. 1956, started at Sainte Marie in 1960 for 'the reliability and quality of its teaching, because it was close to where we lived after we moved, and for the religious training'.

Her sisters went to Sainte Marie, her brothers to Janson de Sailly, to a private school in the Auvergne and to Saint Jean de Passy.

Would send her daughters to Sainte Marie 'for part of their schooling, either at primary or secondary level. It would depend on their nature and ability to adapt as well as on the general quality of education in France at that time.'

Quality: 'coherence and consistency'.

Defect: 'pretending that the world is perfect, just, and good. Ignoring the fights that are a necessary part of existence and the clashes between people.'

Is a member of the old girls' association.

Went on to study politics, law (master's degree), and public affairs. Got her first job in 1980 as 'press attaché, then communications adviser' in a political party.

Father's occupation: management consultant. Mother's occupation: journalist and official representative of the Centre nationale des recherches scientifiques.

Honorine is a spinster.

*Blandine*, b. 1955, started at Sainte Marie in 1968 'because of very poor results at my state school (I had to retake a year) and lack of supervision'. She was the first member of the family to attend Sainte Marie (subsequently a sister and some nieces went there).

Three older brothers and sisters went to state schools.

Has not sent her own daughters to a Sainte Marie college for reasons of geographical distance and because 'everything is going well in the state sector'.

Quality: 'personal follow-through, with each pupil being treated as an individual rather than as a nonentity among a lot of other nonentities. Role of the set mistress.'

Defect: '?'

Not a member of the old girls' association.

Went on to teacher-training college and became a primary teacher in 1977.

Father's occupation: inspector of taxes. Mother's occupation: none.

Blandine got married in church in 1976 after 'a year of living together'; she has three children. Husband a PE teacher and mountain guide.

*Hélène*, b. 1955, started at Sainte Marie in 1960: 'good reputation of the establishment. Closeness to where we lived. Religious education.'

Five younger brothers and sisters. The three brothers completed their secondary education at Franklin, Ecole du Marais. One sister is at business college; the other is at a state school (*lycée* Saint James) in Neuilly.,

Her two daughters attend Sainte Marie de Neuilly.

Quality: 'strictness and high standards'.

Defect: 'a certain lack of flexibility. Pupils have to fit into a very precise mould. "Difficult" characters have to be controlled, taken in hand.'

Is a member of the old girls' association.

Went on to study literature, English, journalism, and communications techniques. Has worked as a 'political journalist' since 1981.

Father's occupation: banker. Mother's occupation: none.

Hélène got married in church in 1976, had two children, and was divorced in 1984. Her ex-husband is an auditor.

*Martine*, b. 1956, started at Sainte Marie in 1966 for 'the quality of the teaching'.

A brother at *lycée* Carnot, then at Sainte Croix de Neuilly college; a sister at Sainte Marie de Neuilly.

Quality: 'methods of work'.

Defect: 'hypocrisy and élitism'.

Not a member of the old girls' association.

Went on to study medicine (Broussais, Paris hospitals); has worked as a hospital doctor since 1979.

Father's occupation: commercial director.

Martine is living with a man but has no children. Her partner has qualifications in business studies and is currently engaged in further study.

*Carole*, b. 1956, started at Sainte Marie in 1970. Previously she had been a pupil at Saint Pie X, where there was no post-16 education. So at 15 she transferred to Daniélou on the advice of the headmistress of the *lycée* Saint Cloud.

Her four brothers went to Franklin, one sister to Pie X and another to Daniélou.

Living in Bordeaux, she would not be able to send her daughters to Sainte Marie.

Quality: '... the attention pupils receive. For instance, I was absent for the first term and the beginning of the second term of my final year for health reasons. The backing of the whole class and of the teachers enabled me gradually to pick up my schooling and get through my school-leaving exam.'

Is a member of the old girls' association.

Carole went on to study medicine (Nanterre, Paris hospitals). She subsequently took a doctorate in medicine, specialising in functional re-education. A hospital house physician from 1979, she has been a deputy head of clinic since 1983.

Father's occupation: engineer.

Carole is living with a man with a view to getting married. No information was given about her future husband.

*Brigitte*, b. 1955, started at Sainte Marie when it moved to Rueil in 1970 (she was one of the new recruits). Reasons: 'eldest of seven children, chance of boarding with cousins in Rueil. Religious establishment and academic standard, particularly as compared to the private schools in Le Havre, where my parents lived.'

One sister completed her secondary education at a *lycée* in Le Havre, three brothers went to Saint Jean de Passy, two other sisters to Daniélou.

If she had daughters of her own, she does not know whether she would send them to a Sainte Marie college.

Quality: 'standard, quality of teaching staff'.

Defect: 'a possibly over-protected environment, despite an ostensible openness to the outside world'.

Not a member of the old girls' association.

Brigitte went on to study medicine in Paris, eventually obtaining a master's degree in genetic bio-chemistry. She completed her studies in 1980 and has been professionally active since that date in the 'techno-business-industrial' field.

Father's occupation: industrialist in Le Havre.

Brigitte had a non-church wedding. She describes her husband as a 'travelling techno-businessman'.

*Nicole*, b. 1955, started at Sainte Marie in 1971: 'adequate schooling, pleasant, new surroundings, openness towards others'.

Her brother went to Saint Jean de Béthune in Versailles (taking his school-leaving exam in 1974), her sister to Sainte Marie (school-leaving exam in 1978).

Nicole lives in Brittany so is unable to send her daughters to Sainte Marie.

Quality: 'openness towards and respect for other people'.

Defect: 'lack of freedom of expression'.

Not a member of the old girls' association.

Nicole went on to study medicine (Necker). A hospital house physician since 1980, she is currently training to specialise in medical re-education.

Father's occupation: engineer. Mother's occupation: none.

Nicole got married in 1982 and has two children. Her husband is a physiotherapist.

*Laurence*, b. 1955, started at Sainte Marie in 1972 for 'continuity of schooling in the private sector and closeness to home'.

If she had daughters she 'would not send them to Sainte Marie particularly but certainly to a private school'.

Quality: 'rigorous teaching (with all that that implies)'.

Defect: sectarianism'.

Not a member of the old girls' association.

Laurence went on to study medicine, subsequently specialising in physiotherapy and acupuncture. A qualified masseuse-physiotherapist and acupuncturist, since 1978 she has been professionally active 'in relation to her studies'.

Father's occupation: company chairman. Mother's occupation: none.

Laurence was single.

*Corinne*, b. 1955, started at Sainte Marie for reasons of 'academic, religious, and moral education'.

Her sisters attended Sainte Marie de Passy; a brother went to a private school in Meudon (Ecole de la Source).

Quality: 'none that I can see'.

Defect: 'lack of openness to life, competitiveness'.

Not a member of the old girls' association.

Corinne went on to study medicine, psychology and nursing; has worked since 1978 as a nurse and psychologist.

Father's occupation: senior civil servant. Mother's occupation: international civil servant (OECD).

Corinne got married in 1982 and has one child. Her husband is a qualified maths teacher currently working as a research assistant.

*Christiane*, b. 1955, started at Sainte Marie in 1963 for 'the quality of the education, both moral and academic'.

An aunt on her father's side had gone there.

Brothers at Gerson and Saint Louis de Gonzague, a sister at Sainte Marie.

Christiane will be sending her children to Sainte Marie from primary age.

Quality: 'respect for others; learning good working techniques'.

Defect: 'a somewhat too over-protected environment'.

Is a member of the old girls' association.

Christiane went on to study medicine (Broussais); she then specialised in psychomotor re-education, obtained a diploma, and practised from 1979 to 1982.

Father's occupation: Bank of France director.

Christiane got married in church in 1979 and has two children. Her husband is a 'product manager' with a diploma in marketing techniques.

*Colette*, b. 1956, started at Sainte Marie in 1970: 'I wanted to leave my state school because I was finding it difficult to do any work there.'

Her brothers and sisters went through school and university in the public sector.

Quality: 'provides a very good all-round culture'.

Defect: 'too sectarian and too BCBG [see footnote above, p. 85]. Very hard to fit in at university after a relatively long period at Sainte Marie.'

Not a member of the old girls' association.

Colette went on to study medicine, later switching to biology and computers. 1978–81, worked part-time for a pension fund; subsequently had a full-time job in computers (middle management).

Father's occupation: consultant engineer. Mother's occupation: none.

Colette got married in church in 1982 and has one child; her husband is a research engineer in computer science.

*Isabelle,* b. 1953, started at Sainte Marie in 1960 because 'it was a private school near where we lived'.

She would send her daughters 'for the early years only'.

Quality: '... high standard of teaching. The subjects are taught by good teachers.'

Defect: 'education too restricted, pupils are over-protected and not sufficiently mixed or warned about life's difficulties, too much academic teaching at the expense of sport or class visits'.

Isabelle went on to study pharmacy and foreign languages (English and Spanish), completing her studies in 1978. Since then she has worked as a bilingual secretary.

Father's occupation: civil engineer. Mother's occupation: none.

Single.

*Muriel,* b. 1955, started at Sainte Marie in 1966 'mainly for the quality of the teaching'.

Cousins of hers went to Sainte Marie; a brother went to Saint Jean de Passy.

Quality: 'it is not just an academic education that is provided there but a moral and religious education as well'.

Defect: 'don't know'.

Not a member of the old girls' association.

Muriel went on to study pharmacy. Since 1980 she has worked as a pharmacist in a laboratory (in her father's company) manufacturing medical equipment.

Father's occupation: company chairman. Mother's occupation: painter.

Muriel got married in church in 1981 and has three children. Her husband, a graduate of the prestigious Ecole centrale des arts et manufactures, is a computer engineer.

*Agnès,* b. 1955, started at Sainte Marie in September 1970: 'The college moving to the western suburbs, my having to repeat a year. Mummy thought I was "right" for it, and I did in fact adapt very quickly.'

Two brothers at the Scelle Saint Cloud *lycée,* a sister at state school, then Daniélou.

Would readily send her children to the Daniélou Centre (too far). Her children attend a private school.

Quality: 'coming from a state school, I was struck by the pupils' general level of culture'.

Defect: 'not so good on the science side'.

Is a member of the old girls' association.

Agnès went on to study pharmacy, obtaining her diploma and working in a hospital from October 1979.

Father's occupation: general secretary. Mother's occupation: pharmacist.

Agnès got married in church in 1979 and has three children. Her husband is a hospital doctor.

*Jeanne*, b. 1954, started at Sainte Marie at the age of 6. Two older sisters tried for the college but were not accepted; a cousin went there for four years. 'The school had a good reputation as regards work and the education provided.'

One handicapped sister went to a special school; one sister at Victor-Hugo, followed by Beaux-Arts; one sister at Maspéro, Mortefontaine, Dupanloud.

Her daughters attend Notre Dame de Chatou and will probably transfer to the Le Vésinet *lycée* next year.

Quality: 'teaching a kind of physical, mental, moral, and spiritual rigour'.

Defect: 'the verso of its quality, sometimes too much rigidity'.

Not a member of the old girls' association.

Jeanne went on to study occupational therapy (Necker), later adding painting, sculpture and Russian iconography. Practised as an occupational therapist for a year in 1977; organised exhibitions of painting in Saudi Arabia in 1986.

Father's occupation: civil engineer. Mother's occupation: bringing up six children!

Jeanne and her physiotherapist husband married in 1976; they have two children.

*Claire*, b. ?, started at Sainte Marie in 1971: 'my parents wanted me to have a religious education'.

Brothers and sisters at Saint Cloud *lycée*, Saint Jean de Béthune, Saint Nicolas de Passy.

Quality: 'choice of teachers'.

Defect: 'lack of openness towards the outside world (all levels of social class)'.

Not a member of the old girls' association.

Claire went on to study medicine, subsequently switching to occupational therapy. She obtained her diploma in 1978 and has practised since that date.

Father's occupation: auditor.

Claire is unmarried and not 'currently' living with anyone.

*Caroline*, b. 1955, started at Daniélou in September 1971: 'We had just moved to the Paris region; the nearest state secondary school (Saint Cloud) had a bad reputation (drugs). So my parents chose the Sainte Marie college.'

Her brothers and sisters went to Catholic schools.

Quality: 'a certain openness'.

Defect: 'too academically oriented'.

Not a member of the old girls' association.

Caroline went on to study nursing, subsequently specialising in nursery nursing. Having nursed for four years, she has been working as a nursery nurse for sixteen months.

Father's occupation: head of a legal firm. Mother's occupation: housewife.

Caroline is single.

*Maryvonne*, b. 1956, started at Sainte Marie in 1963: 'geographical proximity and family tradition, my mother and my aunts went there'.

Her sisters went to Sainte Marie, La Tour, Les Oiseaux; her brothers went to Franklin, Gerson, Saint Jean de Passy.

Maryvonne does not know if she would send her daughters to a Sainte Marie college.

Quality: 'organisation of work, generosity towards others'.

Defect: 'religious education, regimentation'.

Is a member of the old girls' association.

Maryvonne went on to study decorative arts and interior design but never graduated. Has worked as a window-dresser.

Father's occupation: editor. Mother's occupation: none (family belongs to the aristocracy).

Maryvonne got married in church in 1978 and has two children. Her husband is a freelance computer engineer.

*Odile*, b. 1955, started at Sainte Marie in 1958: 'it was the closest to where we lived'.

Her sisters went to Sainte Marie, her brother to Franklin.

Would not send her own daughters to a Sainte Marie college.

Quality: 'solid foundations in French and high standard of general culture'.

Defect: 'everything to do with the psychological and religious aspect'.

Not a member of the old girls' association.

Odile went on to study decorative arts but never completed her dissertation. She has worked as a freelance illustrator since 1979.

Father's occupation: commercial engineer. Mother's occupation: none.

Odile got married in church in 1979 and has two children. Her husband studied political and economic sciences and is a journalist.

*Betty*, b. 1955, started at Sainte Marie de Neuilly in 1962 for 'the quality of study, the guarantee of results, and an *élitist* policy' (her emphasis).

Some cousins went there too.

Her boys attend a private school.

Quality: 'intelligence of the teaching, acquisition of a method of working, high moral and intellectual standard, multi-disciplinarity whatever option was taken'.

Defect: 'only suits brainy girls'.

Not a member of the old girls' association.

Betty went on to do business studies but never took a diploma. She started working in 1974 as a bilingual typist and rose to become 'head of credit control/fraud at American Express'.

Father's occupation: joint managing director of a large company.

Betty got married in 1976 and has three children. She is now divorced. Her ex-husband has degrees in economics and political science and occupies a senior managerial position with Eurocard/Mastercard.

*Pauline*, b, 1956, started at Sainte Marie in 1966: 'advanced sense of education and supervision, religious and moral education going hand in hand, reputedly sound academic standard in arts subjects and in maths'.

She has an aunt who was educated at Sainte Marie and who became a nun, donating a property to the Saint Francis Xavier community.

Her four younger sisters went to Sainte Marie (doctor, nurse, private business college; another sister received part of her schooling at Sainte Marie, then at another private school, and became a speech therapist). One brother at Franklin with a view to going on to either Louis-le-Grand or Janson de Sailly *lycées*.

Pauline is thinking of sending her daughters to Rueil.

Quality: 'good standard, moral values (of conduct: consideration for others, awareness of social and religious problems, openness towards the world rather than cult of self like my children at state school), one breathed religion there like air, it was part of everyday life'.

Defect: 'none as regards content; the set teachers enjoy a level of power well above their IQ (fortunately with some splendid exceptions) and come down hard on the same pupils for several years running; wrongful expulsions higher up the school (on criteria that diverged from the spirit of education)'.

Is a member of the old girls' association and is delighted to receive news of others through *Coup d'oeil* [a leaflet put out by the old girls' association to gather news of old girls and persuade them to join].

Pauline went on to study maths and engineering, specialising in maritime and petroleum engineering. She has worked as a petroleum engineer since 1980.

Father's occupation: engineeer. Mother's occupation: 'bringing up her children (master's degree in law and nursing diploma)'.

Pauline got married in church in 1979 and has 'two children for now'. Her husband is an engineer and economist.

*Frédérique*, b. 1955, started at Sainte Marie in 1965 for reasons of 'closeness to home, religious education, single-sex education, one sister at the college before her'.

Her mother had spent several years at Sainte Marie.

Brothers at Janson de Sailly; one sister at La Tour, another at Sainte Marie. Frédérique has not sent her daughters to Sainte Marie for reasons of geographical distance and disagreement with the education provided.

Quality: 'reliability'.

Defect: 'we were given the impression that we formed part of an élite'.

Is a member of the old girls' association.

Frédérique went on to study English, obtaining a master's degree and a diploma in bilingual teaching. She worked as a bilingual teacher from 1975 to 1977.

Father's occupation: company organiser. Mother's occupation: at home.

Frédérique got married in church in 1975 and has three children. Her husband is a dental surgeon.

*Bérengère*, b. 1955, started at Sainte Marie in 1966 for 'religious reasons'.

Her aunts had gone there before her. Her sisters also went to Sainte Marie, her brothers to Janson de Sailly, Franklin, Saint Jean de Passy.

If she had daughters of school age she would not send them to Sainte Marie.

Quality: 'its methods of work'.

Defect: 'hypocrisy'.

Not a member of the old girls' association.

Bérengère went on to study political science, eventually obtaining a master's degree. Since 1978 she has 'done different jobs in publishing, advertising, press relations'. She is currently 'head of press relations with X consultants'.

Father's occupation: company director. Mother's occupation: none.

Bérengère is single.

*Cécile*, b. 1956, started at Sainte Marie in 1961 'for its religious values and the quality of the teaching'.

Her four sisters also went there, a brother to Gerson.

Quality: 'quality of academic teaching'.

Defect: 'too much comfort, not enough questioning, hence a certain fragility when one is plunged into active life. Absence of co-education. Excessive Parisianism.'

Cécile went on to study politics, law, and journalism and worked as a journalist from 1979 to 1984.

Father's occupation: insurer. Mother's occupation: housewife.

Cécile got married in church in 1981 and has one daughter. Her husband is a pharmaceutical biologist.

*Béatrix*, b. 1956, started at Sainte Marie in 1960 'because of its closeness, religious education, and standard of teaching'.

Her mother and sisters attended the college. Her brother went to Saint Jean de Passy.

Béatrix does not send her daughters to a Sainte Marie college for reasons of geographical distance.

Quality: 'open-mindedness'.

Defect: 'does not leave much time for doing other things'.

Is a member of the old girls' association.

Béatrix went on to study business management and began working as an 'assistant bank manager' in 1979.

Father's occupation: engineer. Mother's occupation: housewife.

Béatrix got married in church in 1982 and has two children. Her husband has a degree in business management and is a financial director.

*Marie-Chantal*, b. 1955, started at Sainte Marie in 1960 for 'a religious education' and because it was 'close to where we lived'.

Her sisters went to Sainte Marie and to Les Oiseaux, her brother to Janson de Sailly and Franklin.

Her children go to a nursery school near their home.

Quality: 'general culture with the accent on literature, learning how to organise one's work in an independent, responsible manner and how to present it both orally and in writing'.

Defect: 'scientific matters. I had excellent maths and physics teachers at Sainte Marie; rather it's the environment that thinks more highly of arts than maths options. These comments relate to what I felt when I finished secondary school in 1973.'

Is a member of the old girls' association.

Marie-Chantal went on to study maths and physics, then statistics and economics, then management. She subsequently obtained diplomas in engineering and at the European Institute of Business Administration. She has worked as an executive at a large industrial group (Matra) since 1978.

Father's occupation: member of parliament. Mother's occupation: picture restorer.

Marie-Chantal got married in church in 1979 and has three children. Her husband has degrees in politcs and law (master's) and works as a financial director.

*Sabine*, b. 1956, started at Sainte Marie in 1966 because 'in my parents' eyes it was the best school locally'.

A sister went to Sainte Marie, a brother to Janson de Sailly.

She might send her daughters there but not before secondary age.

Quality: 'openness and strictness'.

Defect: 'élitism'.

Is a member of the old girls' association.

Sabine went on to higher education and obtained various degrees. She worked from 1978 to 1979 and again from 1981 but does not specify at what occupation!

Father's occupation: construction engineer. Mother's occupation: none.

Sabine got married in church in 1978 and has two children. Her husband is a departmental manager at Peugeot.

*Elisabeth*, b. 1956, started at Sainte Marie in 1960 for 'religious and moral reasons'.

Three sisters were educated at Sainte Marie and La Tour.

For reasons of geographical distance her daughter attends a state nursery school.

Quality: 'religious education and quality of work'.

Defect: 'lack of openness towards certain worlds'.

Not a member of the old girls' association.

Elisabeth went on to study business, obtaining a diploma in 1977, since when she has worked as a sales engineer.

Father's occupation: member of parliament. Mother's occupation: none.

Elisabeth got married in church in 1981 and has one child. Her husband has the same business diploma and is a sales manager.

*Julie*, b. 1955, started at Sainte Marie in 1972, after the college moved to Rueil.

Her brother went to the local primary school and then to private school (Saint Charles de Rueil).

Quality: 'depth of study, emphasis on thinking and private study'.

Defect: 'possibly a certain lack of openness'.

Not a member of the old girls' association.

Julie went on to study law and English but did not obtain a degree. Started working as an administrative secretary in April 1975. Current position: policy inspector.

Father's occupation: technician. Mother's occupation: none.

Julie married in ?. Her husband had no secondary education and is currently working as a driving instructor.

*Clara*, b. 1955, started at Sainte Marie at primary age because it was 'a religious school'.

Sisters at Sainte Marie, brothers at Saint Jean de Passy.

Her daughters do not attend Sainte Marie for reasons of geographical distance; they go the Ecole de la Providence, rue de la Pompe (La Tour).

Quality: 'good work organisation'.

Defect: 'indoctrination'.

Not a member of the old girls' association.

. Clara went on to study law, history, and art history. From 1978 to 1986 she worked as a lecturer for the National Museums.

Father's occupation: manager with the French national petroleum company (CFP). Mother's occupation: executive (aristocratic family).

Clara married in 1979 and has three children. Her husband is an 'assistant manager'.

*Perrine*, b. 1955, started at Sainte Marie in 1961 because 'it was a religious school with a high academic standard'.

A cousin had been there before her.

Her brothers and sisters went to Lübeck and Sainte Croix de Neuilly.

Her daughters do not go to a Sainte Marie college for reasons of geographical distance. They currently attend Sainte Marie de la Madeleine-Fénélon.

Quality: 'thorough subject method'.

Defect: 'insufficient open-mindedness'.

Not a member of the old girls' association.

Perrine started studying law but switched to an executive secretarial college and a British chamber of commerce, obtaining the relevant diplomas. From 1975 to 1977 she was executive secretary with a Canadian stockbroker.

Father's occupation: company director. Mother's occupation: none.

Perrine got married in church in 1978 and has three children. Her husband, a graduate of the European Business School, has an executive position with a bank.

*Sandrine*, b. 1955, started at Sainte Marie in 1962 for 'its high academic standard, the fact that many children of friends were there, closeness'.

Sisters at Sainte Marie and La Tour.

Sandrine would not send her daughters to Sainte Marie.

Quality: 'a very high level of general culture'.

Defect: 'teaching not sufficiently open to the outside world and no preparing pupils for higher education at university or elsewhere. Highly neurotic teachers.'

Not a member of the old girls' association.

Sandrine went on to study art history, law, languages (notably English) and documentation. She has worked since 1979 as an assistant curator in the research department of a Paris museum.

Father's occupation: lawyer. Mother's occupation: none.

Sandrine got married in church ('it would have been hard to say no, we never go to mass') in 1982 and has two children. Her husband, who has a doctorate in tax law, works as an accountant and auditor.

*Françoise*, b. 1955, started at Sainte Marie in 1970, repeating a year before doing her final year (in other words, she was there for three years), for 'qualities of study and education, plus the fact that some old friends of my parents sent their four daughters there, the eldest of whom was a year older than me and was very insistent that I should go'.

'My two brothers received all their secondary schooling at Saint Joseph de Reims. My sister completed hers at Les Oiseaux in Paris.'

Does not know if she would send her daughters to Sainte Marie; 'it's a good thing to have both state and private'.

Quality: 'I was very lucky, quality of supervision, teachers, and pupils'.

Defect: did not reply.

Is a member of the old girls' association.

Françoise went on to study law (Reims) and politics (Paris). Worked from 1976 as an executive assistant.

Father's occupation: managing director of a champagne company. Mother's occupation: housewife.

Françoise got married in church in 1985 but has no children yet. Her husband is still studying for a degree in law.

*Sylvie*, b. 1954, started at a Charles Péguy school at primary age. Her parents were looking for a structured educational environment to offset an exploded family environment.

Her brother attended Saint Jean de Passy.

Quality: 'moral backbone, a certain humanism'.

Defect: 'having been made to stay there throughout my school career, my parents' choice but not necessarily mine'.

Not a member of the old girls' association.

Sylvie went on to study law, switching to medicine after a year and taking a nursing diploma. She has worked as a nurse since 1978.

Father's occupation: sponsorship manager at a large insurance company (UAP). Mother's occupation: general agent for UAP.

Sylvie got married in church in 1975 and has no children. Her husband is a freelance computer programmer.

*Suzanne*, b. 1955, started at Sainte Marie in 1966, 'probably because of the academic standard, which was said to be high at Sainte Marie, plus a certain security as compared to the supposedly decadent world of state schooling'.

Her brothers went to state secondary schools, then to private church schools.

If Suzanne had daughters she would not send them to a Sainte Marie college.

Quality: 'strictness and high standard of teaching staff'.

Defect: 'too slanted towards literary concerns – by too slanted I mean too traditionalist, too turned in on itself socially'.

Not a member of the old girls' association.

Suzanne went on to study economics, politics and architecture, working throughout in a 'construction research office', plus various other jobs.

Father's occupation: 'used to be a printer, now retired'. Mother's occupation: none.

Suzanne is living with a man but supplied no details about him.

*Odette*, b. 1955, started at Sainte Marie in 1964 for 'high standard of teaching, quality of education. Some influence from friends with daughters at Sainte Marie.'

A brother at a state secondary school, a sister at Sainte Marie.

Odette would not send her daughters to Sainte Marie.

Quality: 'competence, strictness, and high standards of the teaching staff'.

Defect: 'absence of coeducation and totally outmoded and anachronistic attitudes of supervision with regard to the male sex (in my day, at least). No initiatives or responsibilities left to pupils, which tends to hold them back in childhood. Too much emphasis on the mind; not enough physical education and sport.'

Was a member of the old girls' association for five or six years but is no longer.

Odette went on to study business management and economics, then psychology and law, specialising in labour law. She has worked as an in-service training manager since 1980.

Father's occupation: representative. Mother's occupation: none.

Odette is living with a man and has one child. Her partner, who has a doctorate in law, is a legal assistant.

*Louise*, b. 1954, started at Sainte Marie in September 1972. 'I went there from another private school at Chatou (Le Bon Pasteur), where I had been for five years; wishing to take a B bac and pass it, the Sainte Marie college doing that option seemed the surest way.'

A twin sister at state school, then at Le Bon Pasteur. Brothers at Saint Erembert in Saint-Germain-en-Laye and Saint Martin de Pontoise, then at crammer.

Louise does not know whether she would send her daughters to Sainte Marie colleges.

Quality: 'pushing pupils to work'.

Defect: 'no obvious fault (only there a year)'.

Not a member of the old girls' association.

Louise went on to study economics and business management, obtaining a master's degree in the latter in 1977, since when she has worked as 'chief product buyer in a purchasing centre'.

Her parents keep a shop.

Louise got married in church in 1983. Her husband did three years at business school and is a sales representative.

*Chantal*, b. 1955, started at Sainte Marie in 1964, her parents having sent her there 'out of concern to give her a religious education and what they considered a quality academic education'. In the circles they moved in, 'everyone sent their children to Sainte Marie, Lübeck, La Tour, or Les Oiseaux'.

Brothers: Franklin, Saint Jean de Passy and Gerson.

Sisters: Sainte Marie and Valmorceau.

Chantal will not be sending her daughters to Sainte Marie because of 'disagreement with the education'. They are at state schools.

Quality: 'learning discipline and how to manage one's work'.

Defect: 'a certain lack of openness towards the outside world'.

Not a member of the old girls' association.

Chantal went on to study economics and business management, obtaining a master's degree in business management and diplomas in accounting and economics and business management. Since 1979 she has worked as a trainee accountant and as a teacher.

Father's occupation: engineer. Mother's occupation: housewife.

Chantal got married in church in 1974 and has three children. Her husband has a diploma in financial management and is a financial executive.

*Nadine*, b. 1955, started at Sainte Marie in 1959 for the 'serious-mindedness of study' there.

Her three sisters were also Sainte-Marie educated.

Quality: 'solid foundations in French'.

Defect: 'having the same maths teacher for four or five years'.

Not a member of the old girls' association.

Nadine went on to study business management, eventually obtaining a master's degree. In 1978 she was a member of a firm of accountants and teaching economics and accountancy.

Father's occupation: company director. Mother's occupation: shorthand typist and graphologist.

Nadine married in 1982 and has one child. Her engineer husband is a project manager dealing with aeronautics.

*Constance*, b. 1954, started at the college in 1965 at the age of 11; for reasons '1) of discipline; 2) of the high academic standard, with religious education included in the curriculum; 3) daughters of friends of my parents were there already; 4) closeness to where we lived (Saint Marie de Passy)'.

Her mother had received her last two years' schooling at Sainte Marie.

Sister: La Tour and Les Oiseaux.

Constance's daughter attends the City of Paris nursery school.

Quality: 'strictness, particularly as regards written work, a big help when it comes to the school-leaving exams. Excellent travel speakers (Rome), walking encyclopaedias.'

Defect: 'at that time the teaching was purely oriented towards the school-leaving exams as if nothing else existed (particularly not a love life, etc.), too closed-in a world'.

Not a member of the old girls' association.

Constance went on to study art history, English, drawing and picture restoring, completing her studies in 1978. Employed as a packer in a textile company from 1977.

Father's occupation: architect. Mother's occupation: accountant since her husband's death.

Constance got married in church in 1978 and has one child. Her husband is a solicitor.

*Blanche*, b. 1955, started at Sainte Marie 'in the very junior classes. Religious education, high academic standard, pupils from the same milieu.'

Sisters: Sainte Marie. Brothers: Sainte Croix de Neuilly. One sister at state secondary school.

Blanche would not send her daughters to a Sainte Marie college.

Quality: 'high standard of schooling'.

Defect: 'lack of openness towards the outside world, narrow-mindedness, authoritarianism, etc.'.

Not a member of the old girls' association.

Blanche went on to study Chinese, breaking off after a year to work as a 'picture restorer'.

Father's occupation: 'inspector of taxes' (aristocratic family).

Blanche got married in church in 1985 and has one child. Her husband, with a degree in sociology, works as a photographer.

*Véronique*, b. 1955, transferred to Daniélou in 1970 'for the academic standard, that of state schools was declining. And maybe the social milieu.'

Her sisters went to private schools.

Véronique would send her daughters to a Sainte Marie college 'if there were one close enough'.

Quality: 'the way each pupil is considered, in other words the opposite of anonymity, plus the open-mindedness'.

Defect: 'certain parts of the religious education'.

Not a member of the old girls' association.

Véronique went on to study maths and physics to master's level. Since 1982 she has been working part-time as a computer engineer.

Father's occupation: doctor. Mother's occupation: none.

Véronique got married in church in 1975 and has two children. Her husband is an engineer.

*Lorraine*, b. 1955, started at Sainte Marie in 1961 'probably because of the guarantee of a religious education and a homogeneous environment'.

A sister at the Institut de l'Assomption, a brother at Saint Louis de Gonzague, two sisters at Sainte Marie.

Would not send her daughters to Sainte Marie.

Quality: 'sensitisation to a certain kind of cultural life thanks to exhibitions, outings, trips, etc.'.

Defect: 'too much intellectualism to the detriment of artistic, manual, etc. skills, which were always seen as inferior, even non-existent'.

Not a member of the old girls' association.

Lorraine went on to study literature and secretarial skills. From 1978 to 1979 she worked in the USA as a French teacher; from 1980 to 1986 she ran a magazine.

Father's occupation: stockbroker. Mother's occupation: none.

Lorraine is single.

*Anne*, b. 1955, started at Daniélou in 1971: 'its reputation for a high level of academic success'.

Her sisters went to Sainte Marie de Rueil and Dupanloud.

Anne has two children, whom she will not be sending to Sainte Marie because of 'educational disagreement'; they attend a private nursery school in Orléans.

Quality: 'general culture, hard work'.

Defect: 'too tram-lined, too sectarian and conformist'.

Not a member of the old girls' association.

Anne went on to study architecture at Nanterre and the Ecole des Beaux-Arts, completing her training in 1980. She practises as an architect.

Anne does not know what her parents trained as.

Her husband attended business school and works as marketing manager for a finance house.

*Marie-Paule*, b. 1954, transferred to Sainte Marie around 1965 for 'the spiritual and intellectual quality, essentially, of the *demoiselles* of Sainte Marie'.

Her four older sisters were already at Sainte Marie.

Her son goes to Saint Jean de Passy, and Marie-Paule intends to send her daughters to a Sainte Marie college.

Quality: 'thorough teaching on solid foundations'.

Defect: 'too much of a Sainte Marie mould, too rigid'.

Not a member of the old girls' association.

Marie-Paule went on to study history, subsequently taking a degree in history and geography. From 1977 to 1982 she worked as a press attaché, from 1982 to 1986 as an advertising manager.

Father's occupation: naval officer. Mother's occupation: none.

Marie-Paule got married in church in 1978 and has three children. Her husband studied politics and business and is now a regional sales manager.

# REFERENCES

Augé, M., 1987, 'Qui est l'Autre?' in *L'Homme*, 103.
Baczko, B., 1984, *Les imaginaires sociaux*, Paris (Payot).
Barthes, R., 1970, *Mythologies*, Paris (Le Seuil).
Beauvoir, S. de, 1958, *Les mémoires d'une jeune fille rangée*, Paris (Gallimard) [Eng. trans. *Memoirs of a Dutiful Daughter*, 1959].
Berl, E., 1931, *Le bourgeois et l'amour*, Paris (Plon).
Bidou, C., Dagnaud, M., Duriez, B., Ion, J., Muehl, D., Pinçon-Charlot, M. and Trecart, J.-P., 1983, *Les couches moyennes salariées, mosaïque sociologique*, Ministry of Town Planning and Housing report.
Bourdieu, P., 1972, 'Les stratégies matrimoniales dans le système des stratégies de reproduction', in *Annales ESC*, 4–5.
    1977, *Le distinction, critique sociale du jugement*, Paris (Minuit, 'Le sens commun').
    1978, 'Capital symbolique et classes sociales', in *L'Arc*, 72.
    1982, *Ce que parler veut dire*, Paris (Fayard).
Braudel, F., 1979, *Civilisation matérielle, économie et capitalisme, XVᵉ–XVIIIᵉ siècle*, vol. II, Paris (A. Colin).
Chartier, R., Compère, M.-M. and Julia, D., 1976, *L'éducation en France du XVIᵉ au XVIIIᵉ siècle*, Paris (SEDES).
Contamine, P., 1976, *La noblesse au moyen-âge*, Paris (PUF).
Cornuel, P. and Duriez, B., 1984, 'La bourgeoisie textile de Roubaix-Tourcoing', in *Revue des cahiers lillois d'économie et de sociologie*, 3.
Coulon, A., 1986, 'Qu'est-ce que l'ethnométhodologie?' in *Ethnométhodologie*, 32–3.
Darnton, R., 1985, *Le grand massacre des chats*, Paris (Laffont).
Daumart, A., 1987, *Les bourgeois et la bourgeoisie en France depuis 1815*, Paris (Aubier).
    1970, *Les bourgeois de Paris au XIXᵉ siècle*, Paris (Aubier).
Duby, G., 1978, *Les trois ordres ou l'imaginaire du féodalisme*, Paris (Gallimard).
    1985, *Histoire de la vie privée*, vol. II, Paris (Le Seuil).
Dupanloud, M., 1880, *La femme studieuse*, Paris (Jules Gervais éditeur).
Elias, N., 1974, *La société de Cour*, Paris (Calman-Lévy).
Engels, F., 1973, *Anti-Dühring*.
Foucault, M., 1975, *Surveiller et punir*, Paris (Gallimard).
Furetière, A., 1981, *Le roman bourgeois*, Paris (Gallimard).
Gay, P., 1984, *The Bourgeois Experience, Victoria to Freud*, vol. I, New York (Oxford University Press).
Goblot, E., 1980, *La barrière de niveau*, Paris (PUF).
Goody, J., 1977, 'Mémoire et apprentissage dans les sociétés avec et sans écriture: la transmission du Bagre', in *L'Homme*, XVII. 1.
Groethuysen, B., 1977, *Origines de l'esprit bourgeois en France*, Paris (Gallimard).
Habermas, J., 1989, *The structural transformation of the public sphere* (translated from the German) Cambridge, Mass. (MIT).

Hahn, A., 1986, 'Contribution à la sociologie de la confession et autres formes institutionalisées de l'aveu', in *Actes de la recherche en sciences sociales*, 62–3.

Halbwachs, M., 1975, *Les cadres sociaux et la mémoire*, Paris (Mouton).

Huppert, G., 1983, *Bourgeois et gentilshommes. La réussite sociale en France au XVIᵉ siècle*, Paris (Flammarion).

Jardin, A. and Tudescq, J., 1973, *La France des notables. La vie de la nation 1815–1848*, Paris (Le Seuil).

Latour, Y., 1975, *Livre de famille*, Dijon (Imprimerie Darantière).

Legendre, P., 1985, *L'inestimable objet de la transmission*, Paris (Fayard).

Léna, M., 1981, *L'esprit de l'éducation*, Paris (Fayard).

Lévi-Strauss, C., 1962, *La pensée sauvage*, Paris (Plon).

1973, *Anthropologie structurale* ii, Paris (Plon).

Le Wita, B., 1984, 'La mémoire familiale des classes moyennes parisiennes', in *Ethnologie française* xix, 1.

1985. 'Mémoire: l'avenir du présent', in *Terrain*, 4.

Le Wita, B. and Sjögren, A., 1987 (a), 'The undefinable bourgeoisie', in *Ethnologia Europea*, xvii.

1987 (b), 'La bourgeoisie, tabou et fascination', in *Les chemins de la ville, Enquêtes ethnologiques*, Paris (CTHS).

Mauss, M., 1968, *Sociologie et anthropologie*, Paris (PUF).

Mayer, A., 1983, *La persistance de l'Ancien Régime*, Paris (Flammarion).

Meyerson, I., 1956, 'Le temps, la mémoire, l'histoire', in *Journal de psychologie*.

Mayeur, F., 1979, *L'éducation des filles en France au XIXᵉ siècle*, Paris (Hachette).

Nietzsche, F., 1882 (revised version 1886), *Die fröhliche Wissenschaft* [Eng. trans. *The Joyful Wisdom*, 1950].

Normand, C., 1908, *La bourgeoisie française au XVIIᵉ siècle*, Paris (Plon).

Peretz, H., 1985, 'La création de l'enseignement secondaire libre de jeunes filles à Paris (1905–1920)', in *Revue d'histoire moderne et contemporaine* 32.

Peronnet, M., 1987, 'Bourgeois, bourgeoisie: les définitions du dictionnaire de l'Académie (1762–1802)', in *Bourgeoisie de province et Révolution*, Grenoble (PUG).

Pouillon, J., 1975, *Fétiches sans fétichismes*, Paris (François Maspéro).

Pourcher, Y., 1987, *Les maîtres de granit*, Paris (Olivier Orban).

Revel, J., 1986, 'Les usages de la civilité', in *Histoire de la vie privée*, vol. iii, Paris (Le Seuil).

Richet, D., 1969, 'Autour de la Révolution française: élites et despotisme', in *Annales ESC*, 1.

Rivière, C., 1983, 'Pour une approche des rituels séculiers', in *Cahiers internationaux de sociologie*, lxxiv.

Sahlins, M., 1980, *Au coeur des sociétés. Raison utilitaire et raison culturelle*, Paris (Gallimard).

Schmitt, J.-C., 1978, 'Le geste, la cathédrale et le roi', in *L'Arc*, 72.

Segalen, M., 1981, *Sociologie de la famille*, Paris (A. Colin).

1985, *Quinze générations de Bas-Bretons. Mariage, parentèle et société dans le pays bigouden sud 1720–1980*, Paris (PUF); Eng. trans., *Fifteen Generations of Bretons*, Cambridge (CUP), 1991.

Sennet, R., 1979, *Les tyrannies de l'intimité*, Paris (Le Seuil).

Sjögren, A., 1986, 'Les repas comme architecte de la vie familiale', in *Dialogue*, 93.

Sperber, D., 1974, *Le symbolisme en général*, Paris (Hermann).

Thélot, C. and Singly, F. de, 1986, 'Racines et profils des ouvriers et des cadres supérieurs', in *Revue française de sociologie*, January–March.

Tollu, F., 1972, *Tableau d'une famille parisienne*, Paris (Beauchesne).

Veyne, P., 1983, *Les Grecs ont-ils cru à leurs mythes?*, Paris (Le Seuil).

Weber, M., 1902–4, *L'éthique protestante et l'esprit du capitalisme* [Eng. trans. *The Protestant Ethic and the Spirit of Capitalism*, 1930].

Zonabend, F., 1980, *La mémoire longue*, Paris (PUF).

1986, 'La mémoire familiale: de l'individuel au collectif', in *Croire la mémoire*, Actes du colloque d'Aoste, 1986.

# INDEX

(Page numbers in *italic* type refer to illustration captions.)

A., family, 140; Mrs Arnold, 11, 45–6, 138
Académie française, dictionary of, 29
Agnès (informant), 149–50
Anne (informant), 161
aristocracy, *see* nobility
*avis* ('Notices'), *see* Sainte Marie colleges

B., family, 140; Mr Charles, junior, 12; Mr
    Charles senior, 12, 46
balls *(rallyes)*, 73, 78, *80*, 81, 115
Balzac, Honoré de (1799–1850), 58
Baraduc's (dancing school), 78–9
Barthes, Roland, and 'name defection', 24,
    40, 52
Baudelaire, Charles (1821–67), 32, 83
BCBG *(bon-chic-bon-genre)*, 85, 148
Béatrice (informant), 143
Béatrix (informant), 153–4
Beauvoir, Simone de, 14, 46, 71, 162
Belleville (district of Paris), 12, 46
Bénédicte (informant), 144
Bérengère (informant), 153
Bergson, Henri (1859–1941), 119
Bernanos, Georges (1888–1948), 39
*Bescherelle* (dictionary; 1864), 25, 28–9, 40,
    45, 55–6; 1858 edition, 39
Betty (informant), 151–2
Blanche (informant), 160
Blandine (informant), 145
Bordeaux, 13
*Bottin mondain, Le*, 62, 78, 127
Bourdaloue, Louis (1632–1704), 51
bourgeoisie (bourgeois), and the Church, 51;
    dictionary definitions of, 2, 23–57, 141;
    diversity of, 1, 4–5, 40–1, 48, 84–5;
    dress habits of, 8, 9, 57, 58, *58*, 59,
    *59*, 62, *63*, 64, *65*, 66–7, 67, 68, *69*,
    88, 115; family memory among, 75,
    118–40; family seats (houses,
    châteaux) of, 3, 17, 32–3, *34*, 35–6, 45,
    126, *128*, 135, *142*; 'middleness'

(median or intermediate position) of, 2,
    17, 25, 49–50; pejorative uses of word,
    25, 53–7; role of women in, 76–7, 82–
    3, 90–1, 92, 95–7; table manners of,
    16, 70–1, 73–7, *77*, 81
Brigitte (informant), 113, 147
Burgundy, 32; see also Minot (Burgundy)

C., Laure, family, 12, 19, 41–4, 46, 129,
    139, 140; Miss Laure, 35; Mrs Laure,
    junior, 12, 19, 43, 105, 113, 129; as
    'ideal type', 90; cited, 46, 78, 101,
    111, 115, 139; dress, 62, 64, 68;
    possessions, 33, 35; Mrs Laure, senior,
    42–3, 45, 60, 129; Mrs Laure, senior
    (grandmother), 126, 129
Camus, Albert (1913–60), 12
capital (capitalist, capitalism), 7, 35, 53–4,
    118, 120
Carnot, *see* Lycée Carnot
Carole (informant), 146–7
Caroline (informant), 101, 106, 113, 114–
    15, 115, 150–1
Catherine (informant), 143–4
Cécile (informant), 153
Chamfort, de (1741–94), 53
Chantal (informant), 105–6, 158–9
Charles Péguy schools, 110–12, 157
Christiane (informant), 44–5, 111, 148
Christine (informant), 94–5
Cicero, 66
Claire (informant), 150
Clara (informant), 155–6
Claudel, Paul (1868–1955), 91
Colette (informant), 95, 107, 113, 148–9
Constance (informant), 159–60
Corinne (informant), 148
Corneille, Pierre (1606–84), 26

D., Jean-Baptiste, family, 12–13, 19; Mrs
    Jean-Baptiste, 12, 35

166